THE ALMOST ISLAND

ATLANTIC CORNWALL

Des Hannigan

DES HANNIGAN

Published by Scryfa of Linkinhorne
scryfa.com
Designed by Simon Parker
© scryfa 2017
© des hannigan 2017
ISBN: 978-1-9997598-0-3
First Published June 2017
Second Impression November 2017
Third Impression June 2018
Fourth Impression May 2019

Cover illustration: The Circle of Life
by the Aegean artist Alexander Reichardt
of Fish & Olive Creations, Halki, Naxos, Greece
(fisholive.com)

FOREWORD

I came into Cornwall in the early 1960s carrying intense memories of Scotland's great hills beyond which I knew little else. I was heading for Germany, the Alps, Greece, anywhere for a change. Cornwall was meant to be a 'diversion'. I am still in Cornwall fifty years later although I have diverted often enough to many other places in the world. Cornwall is my 'home ground', however, and it is the far west of the county and its offshore waters that invest me with intense memories now.

There have been many fruitful associations along the way. During the 1980s, I worked as a journalist for a number of Cornish newspapers and periodicals, work that gave me some knowledge of life, people and events in the county from the everyday to the extraordinary.

In 1987, the National Trust commissioned me to write two booklets about West Penwith as part of the groundbreaking series Coast of Cornwall that described the Trust's coastal properties in the county. I owe a great deal of what I know about the Cornish coast to the boundless research material the Trust gave me access to.

What I know of the sea comes from my years as a fisherman. What I know of the minutiae of the Cornish cliffs comes from thirty years of rock climbing with trusted companions.

A journey through the pages of this book will take the reader from those spectacular cliffs to the lonely reaches of the Celtic Sea in the company of fishermen, lifeboatmen, coastguards, rock climbers, famous writers and artists.

To them all, and especially to old shipmates and climbing mates and to the cliffs and sea, this book is a small hymn of praise and gratitude.

Des Hannigan, Trevowhan, Morvah, 2017

Des Hannigan spent thirty years working for guidebook publishers such as Lonely Planet and AA Publishing covering destinations as varied as Greece, Denmark and Pakistan. He has written many features and books about Cornwall and the Cornish sea including rock-climbing guides to West Cornwall's sea cliffs. Before he became a writer, he worked for fifteen years as a commercial fisherman.

Several pieces in this book were published previously in *Scryfa, Cornish Life*, *The Cornishman*, *Western Morning News*, *Impressions of a Landscape* (St Ives Printing & Publishing Co) and *Atlantic Edge* (Penwith District Council). The verse, *Mer Hunting*, received a Gorsedh Kernow award.

My great thanks to Simon Parker for his fine work on this book and for his encouragement over many years. Special thanks to artist Alexander Reichardt of Fish & Olive Creations, Naxos, Greece for reproduction of his work, The Circle of Life.

THE ALMOST ISLAND

Cornwall has long been described as an almost island linked to the 'beyond' of England by a thread of land. The Elizabethan writer, Richard Carew, put things more elegantly in his *Survey of Cornwall* when he wrote:

> *Nature hath shouldered out Cornwall into the*
> *farthest part of the realm and so besieged it with*
> *the ocean that it forms a demi-island in an island.*

The demi-island metaphor is an apt one. Cornwall does seek to put clear water between itself and England, to strain westwards towards detachment, towards freedom, like a tethered ship eager to let go. The River Tamar defines the Cornwall-Devon border emphatically. It is barely two kilometres across country from the source of the Tamar to Marsland Water, the tiny stream that demarcates the border westwards to the Bristol Channel. Thus, Cornwall is indeed 'almost' surrounded by water. It hangs by a thread of land from Devon's English quayside.

> *In Cornwall, the story goes,*
> *We ride at anchor, always fit to cast*
> *Off from the shores of England.*
> *Especially when an east wind blows.*
> *Then, this little land ship laden*
> *Stands widdershins about.*
> *Not so in westerlies;*
> *Slammed to the bows,*
> *Cornwall lets go all anchors.*
> *She dodges head to wind*
> *Without a backward glance*
> *At that lee shore of perfidy.*
> *One day, she'll make a run for France.*

Carew's characterisation of Cornwall as being a 'demi-island in an island' fits even more aptly the far western peninsula of the county. This is the old Hundred of Penwith, where the final rocky claw of Cornwall thrusts into the Atlantic from between the great bights of Mount's Bay and St Ives Bay to terminate at Pedn an Wlas, the Belerion of the Romans, the Land's End. On Penwith's eastern edge, the low-lying land between Hayle Estuary in the north and Marazion in the south may well have been inundated in the distant past. There are suggestions that Victorian planners considered driving some kind of channel or canal between north and south coasts. This would have made the Land's End Peninsula into an island of sorts. It feels like an island still.

This collection of stories and verses has been inspired by this mere scrap of land, the almost island of Penwith. More precisely, it has been inspired by the great curtain wall of sea cliffs, zawns, promontories, coves and beaches that encloses Penwith, as well as by Cornwall's offshore waters. These extraordinary quarters have been my work place and playground for fifty years. I can do no other than celebrate them in the only way and words I know.

ONSHORE:

NORTH FACING

HAYLE BAR

Hayle Bar is still navigable for a short time either side of high
water although for small open boats it is a mean place in
heavy weather. Boats coming out on a falling tide and in
ground seas have been known to hit the sand with some force.
There is always a final creature wave rising on the outer edge
of the bar where the ground shelves quickly. Just as your
heart is back in place, the edge of the world reappears and
down goes that sinking feeling again. Boats coming in are
sometimes at risk of broaching as the swells overtake them,
the prop bites on thin air, and the vessel starts to swing
side-on to the tumbling sea.

The Cornishman 1985

The north coast of Penwith starts with mud and sand. I
worked out of Hayle for a couple of years in the 1970s netting
for crawfish on the stalwart old boats, *Ocean Pride* and *Our
John*. Hayle was a hard place from which to work. Even on
still mornings as you cruised slowly down river from the
tucked away quietude of the quays, you would see dark lines
of swell beyond the bar and hear the roar of breaking surf on
the sand flats of Porthkidney. The bar would be in full strut, a
brawling heave of ground sea rolling in, green and lovely, not
breaking but silent in itself until the boat began its big dipper
ride, up and over and up and over. Then, she would go down
with a shuddering thud on the hard sand as the next wave
engulfed her, roaring waist deep over the bows and down the
skidding deck until the old boat picked up and climbed
towards the sky once more and the bar spat us out onto the
calming deep of the bay... and so to work.

MORVAH

I live between a rock and a hard place, known also as my own backyard, known also as the parish of Morvah.

Morvah lies on the north coast of the Land's End Peninsula. One meaning of the name is 'by the sea'. Morvah is a very small parish. There are only fifty or so residents. During the mining era of the 1840s, over four hundred people lived in Morvah. The parish boundary is a bare seven miles in circumference. You can walk round it in half a day, mainly on rough rocky ground.

As hard as Morvah Downs is an old Penwith saying – used chiefly by those who do not live in Morvah. Much of the parish is bare moorland studded with rocky outcrops and boulders and the weary bones of prehistoric megaliths. The rest is made up of a mosaic of ancient fields, some with a few tiny settlements scattered among them. These fields are set like emeralds within the silver net of granite 'hedges' that pins the landscape down in this often wind-blasted country. Morvah boasts the highest hill on the Land's End Peninsula, at Watch Croft, 826 feet in height; a Cornish Himalaya. I open my door each morning and there it is; visible on Morvah mist-free days at least.

These rough bounds of Morvah would be diverting enough on their own but the parish has an even more sensational diversion. It is bounded for three miles on its northern edge by one of the wildest stretches of coast in Cornwall, a long series of granite cliffs that rise for nearly three hundred feet to slopes of sweet-smelling grass and wildflowers. From the uneasy base of the cliffs, the Atlantic sweeps majestically towards the horizon beneath an oceanic sky. If Morvah were to be unstitched from mainland Cornwall and spun offshore for a mile or two, it would make a spectacular island. Onshore will do.

Western Morning News 2011

WATCH CROFT

The enfeebled day roared suddenly.
Our boats bent against its flood,
As the hill's green wave
Strained at hard anchors.
Lodged on the high ridge,
A great wind struck,
And the anchors gave.

Then, we feared a fast drift downwind,
To where cities lie in their sumps
In dense Sargassos without tides,
Without the worrying of big winds,
The bite of breaking waves,
Without the blind black night unbarred,
Without the biting blaze of stars,
The hard force of ebb and flood.
No open mouth of water here,
No blade in the blood; no clear air.

This fear was enough
To hold us head to wind,
Until a slow wearing forth
Stemmed the squalling west
And we rode the green wave of the hill
To bring our vessels heeling home to berth.

At Morvah, our weather forecast is written across the northern
sky. No Met Office chart is as graphic as this. Squalls
advance like vast grey barrage balloons. Rain hisses into the
sea beneath them. The sea hackles frantically ahead and is
then hosed flat. We calculate the course of the squalls and
judge whether they will engulf us.

When squalls become full-throated Atlantic fronts, the

Land's End Peninsula buckles down against wind and rain. Morvah bears the brunt. We have a special code for hanging out washing. A one-peg day means a sweet, unthreatening breeze; a two-peg day means brisk winds; a three-peg day means horizontal blasts; a four-peg day is notional; it means a full-blooded Force 8 or 9 gale – with gusts. We would never see our washing again.

MORVAH WASHING

Haul in the sheets and then sheet them in
Before the next fell squall blows out
And takes the loosely-pinned
Into the blazing air and in a spin.
The sea is full of linen;
Lines of foam and fleeces flap
Beyond Manankas and the gap
Of Zawn Alley Isle.
They flit across the sky like semaphore gone wild,
A ragged line of letters single file,
Spelling out the sea's rough lexicon,
Its texts, its tweets, its warning shout,
To haul the sheets in, pin them tight,
Before the next fell squall blows out.

ZENNOR: MER HUNTING

At Zennor, the unseen boundary between the ancient 'country rock' and granite lies two hundred metres inland from the coast. The contrast between these rock types is underlined by the sea-stained cliffs and the silver-grey granite tors that lie bedded amidst gorse and plumed bracken between Rosewall and Zennor Hills. The stone-peppered Zennor Hill was a natural quarry for centuries. Zennor moorstone was used in the building of the tower of St Ives parish church of St Ia. Unfinished blocks of moorstone lie marooned amidst the windblown grass of the hills where the old stonemasons abandoned them. The steep-sided bay west of Zennor Head is Pendower Cove. The sea here can be as smooth as glass in quiet weather. Pendower is enshrined in folklore as the place from where a fanciful mermaid drew down a young chorister whose sweet singing voice had enchanted her. Such myths endure out of fond sentimentality and then become pinned as often tiresome labels on the image of a place. It is Zennor itself, its people and its hinterland, that make the village exceptional.

Atlantic Edge 1995

The Zennor Mermaid is immortalized in a medieval bench end in Zennor's handsome church of St Sennar although there must be a question mark over which came first, the carving or the myth. The stylised mermaid symbol, half fish, half-human, may have been a Christian symbol of Christ's duality yet the pose of Zennor's mermaid reflects the foam-flecked sea goddess Aphrodite. The mermaid's hand-held mirror replaces Aphrodite's bitter quince with a hint of self-regard and a hint of malice. A modern fad for 'Mermaidism' has taken the enduring image of the 'mer' from its darkly erotic traditions as a cruel seducer into a Disneyfied world of kitsch and sentimentality. I have only a cruel response...

MER HUNTING

Baragwanath ate her eyes,
Plucked them clean, as soon as the nets hauled in.
One glance is enough to steal thy soul, he cried.
Gouge them quick, before they swallow thee whole.

We fished for the mer on Sinjan's eve,
When the sea lay mirrored light and brim
With a fuse that ran green through the grain
And the weave of water as clear as gin.

None spoke much on those moon-mad nights
On the sealskin seas of the Long Deep main,
When we shot for the mer and her ilk in the silken light,
Where the mer swung easy on their ropes and chains.

Izzacumpucca was born of a mer. Or so he said.
Born of a Meram and a Bryher man,
Under Hanjague at St Martin's Head,
On a sunder of sand in a cradle of caragheen.

How can you kill your own soul-bred? I asked of him.
A blaze there came from his one good eye,
Like the eye of a mer in the moon-mad night,
In the blood, the blue, and the sea's shot light.

What were the mer but fish-meat to we?
Though sweeter than monk and lobster tail,
Richer than redfish and langoustine.
Their blood as sharp as tin;
As rare as Levantine;
As sweet as sin.

OSBORNE CARN: MORVAH

The streams that run to the sea between Gurnard's Head and
Morvah draw water from the hills of Carn Galver and Watch
Croft. The far west has no rivers to boast of but the liveliness
of every small stream after heavy rain makes up for this.
During the recent wet spell, the rough track that leads down
between the hills was a watercourse in its own right while
everywhere the ground was sodden. February fills the ditches.
Even the low ground below Rosemergy was flooded and the
black walls of Porthmoina Cove were wet leaking. At low tide
a westerly swell broke against the shore and sent spray high
into the air to meet hard winds blowing from the east head on.
The best place to escape an east wind in such weather is
below the cliff tops west of Bosigran. Here, hidden paths lead
between Rosemergy Ridge and Osborne Carn down to grassy
terraces a hundred feet above the sea. Directly below the carn
a jumbled mass of broken slabs and boulders lies close to the
lower adit of Osborne Lode, part of the old Morvah and
Zennor United Mines.

Some time ago, my friend, Tony Bennett, a mining engi-
neer, located this adit. A rock fall had blocked the entrance.
One day we cleared a watery way into the adit and found our-
selves standing ankle deep in running water. On rock shelves,
we found several 'kibbles', iron buckets used for carrying ore
and debris. Though intact, they were so heavily rusted and
oxidised that flakes broke off like piecrust at the merest touch.

One hundred yards into the tunnel, a second rock fall
blocked further progress. A gout of water spouted from the
jammed boulders, indicating that a 'House of Water', a high
build-up lay behind the blockage. This was not the time or
place to unplug the dam. We backtracked, disappointed, to the
open air. All across the slopes water seeped from the ground
and spilled to the shore. To the west, huge seas crashed into
the base of the cliffs in Whirlpool Bay. There has been a great

shifting of sand to and fro along the coast this winter and the beach at Portheras is deep with sand. Whether or not it stays there for the summer is another story.

The Cornishman 1985

AT MORVAH

At Morvah (by the sea) we draw deep breaths.
We keep our eyes wide-berthed
To check the sea's delinquency, its randomness.
There are no cast-off islands here,
No belted reefs to mute the hammer blows
Of the sea's brute force, its high-handedness.
The sea destroys itself at Morvah,
Offloads spume and salt on the frantic wind,
While clouds like Himalaya muster on the rim
Of the Atlantic's taut horizon.
This is a berth to brace against the storm,
When Cornwall dips and slides
Beneath the blows of the earthshakers
And rocks root down to the widowmaker.

PORTHMEOR COVE:
GURNARD'S HEAD

The valley that runs down to Porthmeor Cove is deeper than it seems. The fall of water that drains from the high ground of Porthmeor Common and the rocky summit of the Galvers once powered a water wheel at the old mine workings on the western slopes of the valley. The bones of dressing floors, drains and buddles are still visible amid the grass and there are signs that a calciner once operated here. The complex was part of the Carn Galver Mine, a short-lived venture that closed in 1874. The ruins of the mine's engine houses stand by the roadside a few hundred metres to the south-west, iconic punctuation marks for tourists.

Midway along the cliffs on the eastern side of Porthmeor Cove, a cupola, an intrusion of granite amid the metamorphosed killas and greenstone, breaches the darker rock. The cupola is of great scientific interest to geologists. In fine sunsets, it shines with unscientific light amid the darker rocks.

Porthmeor is a fine place to be in early June. The eastern slopes that lead round towards Robin's Rocks are dense with flowers. Ling is just showing and the first red veins of dodder are weaving their parasitic webs across the gorse. From Porthmeor, the land rises through rough country to Bosigran Farm and its relics of ancient field systems. Beyond all of this, Carn Galver dominates the skyline, rugged and mountainous in form if not in bulk.

There are few places in West Cornwall with such a breadth of open country. Today the skies were hard and clear in the easterly wind although the sea had a summer look to it, unruffled in the lee of the wind and turquoise in the inshore shallows.

Offshore, the newly built fishing boat, *Sweet Promise*, latest in a long line of elegant vessels, powered its way past the huge undercut cliff of Carn Gloose.

Impressions of a Landscape 1987

The preceding piece was a favourite of the poet W. S. Graham; Sydney Graham as he was known, although there were other epithets for that tough, intimidating *makar* of fine words and bad behaviour. Graham's great work was the poem *The Nightfishing*, recognised as one of the best long poems of the 20th century.

Sydney was not a 'career' fisherman, if career is the right word for such a rough old trade. As far as I knew, he had been out on occasions with Mevagissey pilchard men when he lived in the area. From these experiences, *The Nightfishing* had evolved through the remarkable 'lens' of Graham's language. Once, I asked Sydney, out of genuine curiosity, from where he had fished in the Western Isles. Hebridean locations are mentioned in *The Nightfishing*. He sank me with a trademark W. S. Graham look and turned his great leonine head away with haughty disdain, as if avoiding a bad smell.

'Ye'll need tae ask Nessie about that...'

Nessie Dunsmuir, Sydney's guardian wife, rescued me in her kindly way.

'Sydney did not fish in Scotland, m'dear. It's called poetic licence...'

You can see where I was going wrong with Sydney Graham. I was on the periphery of his world, but I met him quite often and even drank with him on occasion. We were at odds. I expect he thought I was an irritation, a mere upstart. Being a fellow Scot did not help me; being a pretend poet likewise; being a full time fisherman even less so.

Sometimes, after drinking sessions at Botallack with the artist Roger Hilton, Sydney called in to my old caravan at Trewellard on his way home along the rolling Cornish road to Madron. He toppled in rather than called in; roared in even. He would demand that I read him my latest sad scribblings and would then, with furious contempt, denounce them as juvenile rubbish. He was right, of course. Eventually, I stopped trying to write until the author Denys Val Baker drew me with kindly encouragement into his *Cornish Review* magazine. Even a slight verse or a very short story would earn a little Celtic cheque of half a guinea from Denys. He was a lovely man who stuck with the life of a writer and stood up for the rights of other writers.

A kindly postscript to Sydney Graham's scornful critique came many years later when I had become a professional scribbler. Very close to death, Sydney sent me a letter praising my writing and expressing his pleasure with my piece about Porthmeor Cove, a place that he had loved and where he wanted to be. Funny old souls, writers…

More Than Conquerors

The coastline from St Ives to Zennor Head weaves in and out of those narrow rocky chasms called zawns, once described tellingly as 'yawns in a cliff'. The rock here is not the ubiquitous golden granite of the tourist brochure. Igneous intrusions transformed the more ancient country rock into dark multi-hued sheets of slate and greenstone. Only at Wicca Pool, a mile northeast of Zennor Head, is the underlying granite exposed, most strikingly in the shape of Wicca Pillar, a sixty-foot column of granite with its feet in the tide. Along the foreshore, the dark rocks are sleek as sealskin where they protrude from a swirling Sargasso of thongweed and bladderwrack. The cliffs are patched with dripping sedge, bright green against the dark rock; on the cliffs, paint-like smears of birdlime drain from the nesting ledges of shags and fulmars. The sea here is rarely at ease.

Atlantic Edge 1995

Wicca lies on one of the loveliest parts of Penwith's north coast. It can be forlorn at times. There have been grim events. There is a discreet memorial at a remote point inland from the coast path. It is not easily seen; a simple bench of granite inscribed with a quote from *Romans 8:37*,

More than conquerors

The inscription commemorates the death by drowning in July 1988 of a father and his adult son, holidaymakers for whom this coastline was well known and loved. They died while fishing from sea level rocks; a younger son survived. The memorial lies high above the shoreline in a setting of peaceful beauty, a serene viewpoint amid wildflowers and granite.

I spoke to the survivor a few hours after the tragedy;

interviewed him rather. I was doing my job, if you could call it that, pursuing a news story of harrowing detail. It was one of the worst things I have ever done. I had been detailed to find 'human interest' for the front page lead of a newspaper. This is the justification for such intrusion. Drama, the 'cruel sea', the shock of such tragic deaths, a brutal contradiction among the beauty and splendour of Cornwall's iconic coast-line. 'Human interest' is the worst justification for such an intrusion. A humane reluctance was more my sentiment. I procrastinated that day. I joined the coastguard team and locals, most of whom I knew well. I clambered about the base of the shoreline cliffs for an hour or two in search of the worst and then, reluctantly, on leaden feet, sought out the nearby cottage where the survivor and his family gathered in their terrible grief. As is often the case with victims of such desperate loss, the young man, the bereaved son and brother, wanted to speak to me, eager to explain, to mourn his loss, to assuage distress somehow, although his comforting family and friends quite rightly resisted me at first with barely concealed loathing.

My only justification was that I put everything I could of compassion into the report I filed. Some weeks later, having read the report, the family wrote to me thanking me for my 'thoughtfulness'. I felt thoughtless still. In those days as a news reporter I often exposed, with some success, cover-ups, bullying landlords, fraudsters who absconded with charity money, businessmen and petty politicians who cheated and dissembled. At times, this was done at the discreet behest of the authorities, or of whistleblowers who could do nothing through official channels. It was considered laudable, of course; the 'power' of even the provincial Press. None of this excused the intrusion that came with the pursuit of survivors of the sea tragedies that were often the default of Cornish news reporting.

I am reminded of this whenever I pass the memorial stone on the occasionally forlorn yet beautiful coast at Wicca. For a moment or two, even beneath a summer sun, darkness falls.

Shaking Hands
With The Devil

Everywhere along Cornwall's corrugated coastline there are
tipping points beyond which you proceed either at your peril
or in control. Like the safety lines clearly delineated a few
feet in from the edge of railway station platforms, this tipping
point of the Atlantic edge testifies to limitations of sense and
safety.

Abseiling down a cliff is controlled falling. Few rock
climbers enjoy abseiling; it is merely necessary. The fashion
for 'charity' abseiling is admirable, but it is understandably
contrived. Sensibly, those brave people who abseil down the
local multi storey car park for good causes are backed up with
a secure safety rope.

Abseiling, as a necessity in climbing, is accomplished
without an additional safety rope. It is controlled falling. The
climber controls the descent through a device clipped to the
abseil rope and to a waist harness. Other devices can be used
as fail-safe brakes if something goes wrong but more often
than not a climber simply zips down the abseil rope, in
control though not necessarily enjoying a process that gets
you to where you climb back up again. It is not worth
questioning the illogicality of this.

Zawn Duel, the 'Devil's Zawn', a huge rocky gash in the
cliff, lies at the heart of the coastal wilderness between
Gurnard's Head and Carn Gloose. It is the deepest zawn in
West Cornwall. Walkers on the coast path stroll by within
yards of the head of Zawn Duel. All they see is the beginning
of a grassy trench that slides seawards, steepening all the
time. Out of sight from above, the trench becomes a deep
ravine whose sheer walls drop nearly three hundred feet to sea
level.

In 1974 , two of the South West's pioneering rock
climbers, Pat Littlejohn and Keith Darbyshire, abseiled into
Zawn Duel from the upper cliff and climbed a hard route on

the west wall. They called it *The Adversary*. It was next climbed in 1976. No one was queuing for Zawn Duel.

In 1994, on a May afternoon full of sunlight and still air, I abseiled into Zawn Duel with Mike Raine, a greatly experienced Yorkshire climber who was teaching in Camborne at the time. We used a 300-foot static line that took us with our climbing ropes and gear to a tiny ledge ten feet above low water mark. The final fifty feet of descent was below an overhang so that we hung in mid-air and, at the last, had to swing in to reach the ledge; an abseil into the afterlife.

Through the gloom, I could just see a narrow tongue of smooth water that licked outwards to where, distantly, the sun blazed on a calm sea. High above us a golden thread of sunlight lay along the eastern rim of the zawn. Our only escape was to climb back up the great cliff although it did cross my mind that we could always swim out. The same thought struck Mike as he spun slowly below the overhang.

We uncoiled our ropes and checked our gear in graveyard silence. It took several hours of intense lead climbing on Mike's part to unlock the problems of *The Adversary* and get us back to the golden light at grass. Later we sat silently in a crowded Gurnard's Head pub, oblivious to our surroundings, staring at the floor as we slowly re-hydrated. A clear space seemed to expand around us.

This was only the third ascent of *The Adversary* in twenty years. Zawn Duel still lies somewhere at the back of my mind. I fetch it out now and then, when I think that life is getting too easy.

At The Seaside

In Zawn Duel, by Gurnard's Head by Pedn Kei,
The light resolves,
Into darkness, thick, blood-black,
Reforms to jet and then dissolves.
We fell from grace and the golden light
To midday's midnight
In one long glide;
An abseil into the afterlife, at the seaside.
Three hundred feet we fell
Between those adamantine walls,
Two madmen in control
Of nothing more than gravity and gall.

The deep zawn stood a bare three fathoms wide.
Its shrouded nave
Echoed to the roar of ocean swells,
Whose driven, distant waves
Struck other canyons and cathedrals drowned.
It shuddered with the sound
Of shoaling fish, a million strong.
They turned on the tide, struck ground,
And where we lodged in Zawn Duel's undercroft,
We felt the lifeblood
Of that undersea, its tides, its legions
Raging towards the flood.

All we had for favour shone,
A beam of golden light at grass. Enough
To draw us up the savage rock
That soared, implacable, above.
We checked our gear;
Then spun our rocky rope trick to the sky.
The neat pavane of climbing's futile dance,

The game of gravity defied.
We rose with grace to the golden light.
A half tide's turn it took to pass
From Zawn Duel's deadly artifice,
To climb that hooded wall to grass.

HALLDRINE COVE: ZENNOR

Halldrine Cove lies just north of the mighty Bosigran Cliff. It is a beautiful place, if you are content with a glorious chaos of rock rather than a beach. The back floor of the cove is crammed with sea-stained boulders. The east and south walls are made up of dark granite covered in sedge and lichen.

Golden cliffs rise on the north side and deep water fills the cove at all states of the tide. The sea is a turquoise colour where it lies above sand. When the sea is rough, Halldrine is a roaring cauldron.

North of the main cove lies a rocky foreshore that spills down to the sea on either side of a deep cleft. On the floor of the cleft, huge boulders, rocked by storm seas, have ground into the bedrock like diamond drills. This area of rock covers a hard acre yet it lies at a gentle angle. It is like a cliff that has been knocked flat. You can walk across the tilted rock and clamber down into the cleft, bridging carefully between its walls above those great grinding boulders within their pools of trapped seawater. The shaped hollows are furred with purple and red coralline algae.

Last weekend, a leaden sky cast gloom over all; yet, there was a depth of tone and texture to this rocky arena that was matched by the rust-red bracken and grass of the slopes above. Low cloud streamed endlessly overhead, ragged and pearl-grey and brooding black to the north.

The wind was bitter. A sullen sea rolled into the cliffs. Each wave exploded in fountains of spray against the great fist of Castle Rock below Bosigran Head. The sea was chaotic within the cove. It looked bitterly cold. Far offshore, pale shafts of sunlight turned the sea to ghostly silver beneath breaks in the cloud.

The Cornishman 1986

Halldrine has all the features necessary for the work of Cornish painters; colours that change with the weather and the sea's mirrored light. The boulders and pinnacles to the east of the cove are as sculptural as anything you might see in a Hepworth piece, although I may be fairly pilloried for saying so.

Within Halldrine are the lineaments of the later St Ives School of Lanyon, Heron and Frost, of Lanyon's immersive take on the Cornish landscape in particular. The rough bounds of coast and moorland exhilarated Lanyon, especially the coast that unfurls from the svelte sands of St Ives towards the west through a satisfying chaos of cliffs and coves. He was an enthusiast for full on engagement with the very fabric of the landscape. He embraced the wildness of the Cornish climate and empathised with the lives of miners, farmers and fishermen; miners especially. Halldrine for me is a quintessential Lanyon construct.

Patrick Heron was more fastidious and cerebral than Lanyon in some ways. Like Frost, he was a supreme colourist; all those sub-fusc almost sepia tones of such Lanyon masterpieces as *St Just* and *Porthleven* would not suit. Heron took deep inspiration from the Penwith landscape and sea but his great inspiration came from celebratory colours such as those of his garden at Eagle's Nest, his fine house above Zennor. Lanyon could paint in brilliant optimistic colour also but his eye was for the darker realism of the cliff, the mineshaft and the winter sea.

Bosigran

and Arthur Westlake Andrews

The great cliff of Bosigran is the seaward extension of a particularly beautiful part of Penwith's north coast. Located between Gurnard's Head and Morvah, the cliff is the exposed end of a massive wedge of granite that reaches its highest point on the rocky outcrops of The Galvers, the attractive rocky hills above the coast road and the twin mine stacks of the old Carn Galver mine.

The old Count House of the mine has been associated with the Climbers' Club of Great Britain for nearly eighty years. The Climbers' Club owes its unique association with Cornwall to the Victorian/Edwardian mountaineer Arthur Westlake Andrews (1868-1959) who lived from 1922 until his death at what had been the Old Poor House by Eagle's Nest (owned by Andrews' uncle) on the high ground above Zennor.

Arthur Andrews was a geographer and athlete (he competed at Wimbledon in 1901). He was also an accomplished mountaineer and rock climber and is recognised as 'the father of sea cliff climbing'. Sea cliffs were seen as mere training grounds for the Alps by early mountaineers, but Andrews recognised how a sea cliff such as Bosigran had natural features of crack, corner, chimney, flake and open face which, when linked together as a 'route' would produce unique climbing. A precedent had been set in 1858 by the Alpinist and literary critic Sir Leslie Stephen, father of Virginia Woolf, who lived in St Ives for a time. Stephen recorded his 'gangling and prehensile' climbing of a chimney in the seaward point of Gurnard's Head.

Arthur Andrews began the development of Cornish climbing. With his redoubtable sister, Marian Elizabeth, known as Elsie, he climbed various routes on Wicca Pillar and in 1902 was the first to climb Bosigran Ridge (later known as Commando Ridge), the great cockscomb of granite that rises for over 700 feet from the sea opposite Bosigran

Cliff; an Atlantic Alpine experience enjoyed by possibly thousands of climbers since.

Beyond the ridge is Bosigran Great Zawn, a hidden fastness that can be viewed properly only from the sea or from its remote western edge. It is a savage place; a great roofless chamber of granite whose opposing cliffs are nearly three hundred feet high. They stand only a few metres apart at the zawn's seaward end. Few seabirds nest here and even daylight has trouble getting in. You can enter Great Zawn only by abseil rope from its landward edge or from the lip of its seaward cliff. The zawn is the site of some of Cornwall's most famous rock climbs but no climber goes near the place without experience and proper equipment. The rewards are worthwhile.

Great Zawn may not have been explored until the 1920s. There are no obvious signs of even the most resourceful of the 'old men' of Cornish mining having visited this granite fastness, although you never know. In 1923, however, the remarkable Arthur and Elsie Andrews searched out the zawn's secrets. The Andrews nursed the exciting, if eccentric ambition of traversing the entire coastline of Britain between high and low water marks. This was a touch unrealistic for one pair of lifetimes but they did manage to traverse the often precipitous shoreline for most of the way from Zennor to Pendeen.

Bosigran Great Zawn was a major challenge; yet Elsie and Arthur managed to cross the awesome northern wall of the zawn by first leaping on to the narrow Green Cormorant Ledge, an achievement that is still a nerve-wracking challenge to modern rock climbers. Elsie was the swimmer of the team. If the pair could not climb round the walls of a sea-breached zawn she would swim across with a rope between her teeth and rig a traverse line in mid-air so that Arthur could haul himself across carrying the picnic.

Arthur Andrews was an accomplished writer and poet. He wrote the first climbing guide to Penwith, published in 1950. It is a unique book, at once informed and literary in style, and is more about the natural world of the cliffs and moors than it is about climbing. The 'guide' features only a few dozen climbs existing at the time. Andrews' poems are hymns of praise to the great cliffs among which he moved with ease and constant delight. I have written subsequent guidebooks to the Penwith cliffs but in the dry functional style required by the modern sport and by the need to cata- logue the many hundreds of climbs now recorded on the great cliffs.

Arthur Andrews was still wandering about the cliffs in his early-eighties, his enthusiasm for the wild places of Penwith undimmed. He died, aged ninety, in 1959. Elsie died in 1977, aged ninety-five. In many ways they had the best of it.

FLOOD TIDE, BOSIGRAN

Tonight the clattering stones stood still,
The wind eased, slack tide held sway,
The air unravelled, ebbed, gave way.

Granted an hour of this paralysis,
I stepped beneath Bosigran's hooded swags,
Picked through the clitter of its bones
Until the moon embarked, let loose the drags,
Leaned to its grunting chains and then,
Unshipped the warps and hauled the tide.

The air fused bright above the cove,
Porthmoina's crest flared with light.
The sky thickened, the sea began its run.
It drove a brisker temper when the moon hooked on,
As, sudden then, the world spun.

A Clockwork Orange:
Long Carn and Rosemergy Towers

Above Great Moor Zawn and Brandy's Zawn on the Morvah coast, ribs of granite protrude from the upper slopes of the cliff at Osborne Carn and Rosemergy Towers. Lichen and ivy cling to the grey rock. At Rosemergy Towers a huge slab of granite has split from the main mass of rock and now rests at a gentle angle. It forms an open-ended cave between itself and the main cliff. The feature is known as Church Cave and is said to have been the chosen meeting place of a group of dissenting Methodists during the late 19th century. Last Sunday, the first proper storms of the coming winter had blown away the late Indian summer and the Towers and their church-like cave roared with a salty wind that was sucked upwards from the tilted cliff below.

Atlantic depressions are tracking farther south now after several weeks of high pressure and with this sea change the colour and texture of the land prove the late hour. Broad swathes of bracken bled into the dark grass of the lower cliff and beneath a lowering sky the sea was like gunmetal except where waves broke offshore and white water flared against the shoreline.

At the mouth of the great cave-cleft of Rosemergy Towers, the sense of height and distance was intense. Below here, the bracken-covered slopes pitched suddenly into thin air. White water laced the tide line where the long reach of cliff from Trevean to Tregaminion and Chypraze curved to the west. Far offshore, dark anvil-shaped clouds built across the sky and in the gathering dusk, the air above the cliffs was full of the smell of rain and damp earth and a winter sea.

The Cornishman 1986

Sometime last century (circa 1985), the late great novelist, Anthony Burgess, came to Cornwall. The air turned blue (Burgess could swear with Shakespearean fluency). The bad language was due to Burgess's irritation with a television crew from Thames TV's *South Bank Show* that was filming a series about famous living writers talking about famous dead writers. They had lined Burgess up for the D H Lawrence slot. Where else but Penwith's north coast for location-location, given Lawrence's sojourn at Zennor during the First World War; given also the splendour of the Cornish land and sea.

I was a humble news reporter at the time. I was also writing an increasing amount of humble narrative about the rougher edges of the Cornish coast. Occasionally someone would give my name to big time writers and filmmakers who were cobbling up pieces about West Cornwall and needed some local help. The *South Bank Show* (aka The Melvyn Bragg Show) hired me for the Burgess/Lawrence filming as a 'location fixer' and half-hearted 'safety adviser'. A gofer by any other name but with very good money to gofer all the same. The whole show was being run, on behalf of the Mighty Melvyn, by a young woman who was hugely professional as well as hugely pregnant. She was hugely undaunted frankly, even by Anthony Burgess who was in something of a grump from the word go.

I got lucky; Burgess and I took to each other immediately. Two grumps together. As soon as we met in the Queen's Hotel, Penzance – where else in the absence of a Ritz? – Burgess dragged me aside and started to complain, in fluent Anglo Saxon, about television, television crews, television programmes and, again, television. I had only heard such fabulously inventive cursing from certain trawler skippers.

Burgess was, however, in a profane league of his own. In the foyer of the Queen's Hotel, Burgess's wife, Liana, the Italian translator and literary agent, and fierce protector of the Burgess Grail, fussed round Anthony with almost maternal affection.

She took to me as well, I'm pleased to say. I was being doubly recruited beyond my brief. Mrs B had decided that since there was no way she was going to traipse about the Cornish cliffs, I was to be Anthony's *guardia del corpo*.

'You must watch his every moves, my dear young mans!' Mrs B said. 'Do not let him fall into the seas! And do not let him smokes too much!'

This last was definitely beyond my brief. Burgess smouldered in every way. As we headed off on location, he gripped my arm.

'Stay close to me,' he muttered. 'You and I must at least remain fucking sane.'

I had suggested a spot on the Morvah coast just west of Rosemergy Towers as being a reasonably accessible cliff-top location for a Burgess-to-camera session. This was the rocky outcrop of Long Carn in the shadow of Watch Croft, Penwith's highest hill. To either side of Long Carn, steep vegetated slopes and granite cliffs tumble down for several hundred feet to the sea. I doubt that Lawrence ever crouched in gloomy reflection there.

The coast path at Long Carn is quickly reached from the road and, although a short section of the path is seeded with boulders, the flat-topped rocks on the summit of Long Carn made an ideal location for the camera team – and for John Anthony Burgess Wilson, to give him his proper name. The day was perfect; the cliffs were at their sun-blitzed best beneath a blue sky. Lazy swells rolled across the sand in the bay below Long Carn and broke in ribbons of white against the granite shore.

We coaxed the camera team and equipment, including Burgess, down to Long Carn without mishap. Burgess was formidable when performing to camera. He perched himself on a convenient throne of rock with his back to sea and sky. The crew fluttered, fixed, focused; they became still as stone as Burgess launched forth. Unscripted; not a word out of place; not a pause; no retakes. Just a fabulous flow of mellifluous flummery about David Herbert Lawrence.

Midway through filming, one of the area's resident peregrine falcons (celebrities in their own right in those days) zipped by and then curved back to hover directly behind Burgess's head from where it cast an imperious sideways glance at the interlopers. The camera crew were transfixed by the falcon but kept rolling. Burgess droned on, unaware that for once an even more formidable raptor was upstaging him. When he finished, the entire team packed up and shot off back to the road babbling about that 'amazing bird' and congratulating themselves on such a good wrap. I was left to escort a wheezing, cursing, panting, and blaspheming Burgess across the fang-like boulders and up the steepish path.

'You should stop smoking,' I said.

'I will when I'm fucking dead!' came the relatively robust reply.

At his peak, Burgess is said to have smoked eighty cigarettes a day. Sadly, he died, aged 76 in 1993, unsurprisingly perhaps, from lung cancer.

Postscript: Years later, the pioneering Devon rock climber Pete O'Sullivan and I tackled the high granite cliff in the zawn directly below Long Carn to produce a long and fairly challenging rock climb that is still a target of visiting climbers today. As is the way with the eccentric pastime of climbing, the lead climber of a new route gives the climb its name. Peter had been reading Anthony Burgess's novel, Earthly Powers and so he called the climb 'Earthly Powers'. Peter knew nothing of my brief shoulder rubbing on the coast path with the mighty Burgess himself all those years before, so there was a pleasing serendipity about the coincidence. I like to think that Burgess might have cherished the obscure detail of having an obscure rock climb on an obscure sea cliff in far Cornwall named after one of his great clockworks.

LONG CARN: MORVAH

At Long Carn, I pilot the sea above deep zawns.
The Atlantic lies in my cupped hands;
An ocean caught in one drop elusive.
This bead-like drop once circled the Aegean,
Swirled east and then west, until,
Pressed between the shoulders of Africa and Andalus,
It found the Mare Glaciale.

Thus, from the Mediterranean,
An ancient Truth was carried north through Biscay
To a cold mirror of the Cornish sea at Morvah.

Long Carn is a place of icon-bearing ways,
A place of Truth and certainties.
Such Truth thrives on lean hard ground.
Its anchor grips the roots of mountains,
The rocky veins of the Atlantic's undersea.

When Long Carn and its zawns lay complete,
When the makers hoisted megaliths at Chun,
The megalith was commonplace in Crete,
The Minoans wrought under the same sun and moon.

There is scant profit in such ancient memories;
The mantras of change and novelty rule us now.
We are overwhelmed.
I know this; I embrace the new.
Yet, here, on Long Carn's prow,
This bead of ocean in my hands holds ancient Truth.
I cleave to that with certainty.

PORTHERAS: BLINKER'S BED

Chypraze Cliff lies to the north east of Portheras Cove at the heart of a remote stretch of the Land's End Peninsula's north coast. Even the coastal footpath gives Chypraze Cliff a wide berth and keeps to the edge of the fields inland.

This is frontier country, where the grassy slopes slide helter-skelter down to the edge of the cliffs. Boulder beaches lie along the foreshore for over a mile between Blinker's Bed and Zawn Alley Isle. At Blinker's, a rocky promontory juts into the sea. With care, you can scramble on to its outer pinnacle when the sea is quiet. From here, you look back into a vast amphitheatre of shattered cliffs where undercut caves and clefts drip constantly with the water that drains from the deeply vegetated slopes above. The shrill screams of seabirds echo from cliff to cliff. A gloriously wild coastline runs for several miles to the north east below the rocky hills of Watch Croft and Carn Galver. There are no fields or farms visible; no roads, no houses. In view are only sea, cliffs, and rough country all the way to Gurnard's Head.

Most of the rocky headwall at Chypraze is unstable, as if the once-molten granite had bubbled over at the edges and frothed full of air. Walls of brittle rock have been honed into fantastic shapes. Black pillars and ochre-stained slabs rise in a series of short steps on either side of the promontory where the sea has hammered and shaped the lower cliff. A short down-climb or abseil lands you on the rocky beach east of the promontory from where you can explore the long reach of coast running towards the small promontory of Zawn Alley Isle, but only at low tide. The flood comes in quickly here. Midway along the beach, a large rock protrudes from the earthy lower cliff. It is like the head of a huge horse, a surreal piece of natural art that stays in my mind.

This coast has been in the lee of southerly winds during the past few weeks but last Sunday the west reasserted itself and the Atlantic reached in with massive ground seas. There was no white water breaking offshore but where the swell collapsed against the base of the cliffs, the sea tore itself apart and sent spray drifting for hundreds of feet into the air. In such conditions it is wise to take the long view of Blinker's and Chypraze from the safety of the upper slopes where leaves of scurvy grass and sea beet gleam wetly in the sun as veils of spray drift along the cliff's edge shimmering with rainbow colours.

The Cornishman 1986

THE FALL

Below the cliff edge,
Below the dripping sedge and grass,
We sense the tipping point, the point of fall;
The place where careless feet give way
And slide, and take us with them, overall.

PENDEEN:
GOLDSWORTHY ZAWN

Between Pendeen Lighthouse and Levant Mine, tinners have
worked the wrenched landscape to the limit. The cliffs here
are mainly killas, the ancient metamorphosed slate known as
'country rock'.

The upper cliff north east of Levant is a chaos of shale
and clinker that spills down the gullies and the lower slopes.
The outfall from Geevor Mine, thickened with iron oxide,
stains the sea blood red for a hundred yards offshore. There
must be a small fortune in ore-bearing silt on the seabed here.
Tonic water also: some of the finest lobsters you'll ever see,
black-backed and red-jointed, are hauled from this ground
where the vicious tides that rip past Pendeen Watch, and
across the offlying rocks of Three Stone Ore, make hauling
pots a hard business. Skin-divers once harvested crawfish by
the sackful around Three Stone Ore.

This cliff is unlike any other in West Cornwall. Below
the old winding gear of the Goldsworthy Shaft there is a deep
and narrow zawn. A gaping adit pierces the back wall. The
west face of the zawn is like an artist's palette, thick with
green cuprous stains, white kaolin and the burnt umber
smears of iron oxide; the antithesis of picture-postcard
Cornwall. Yet, it is far too striking to be called ugly.

Cornish Life 1987

BOTALLACK ZAWN

The coast from Carn Vellan to Kenidjack Castle is cross-grained to the northwest. The cliffs rise in steps from the shoreline and the zawns below Botallack, Wheal Cock and Stamps-an-Jowl are deep, narrow and sunless.

Botallack Zawn is the black heart of hidden Cornwall. It is accessible at low water if there is no swell; but even when the sea is slight, you can still get a faceful of the Atlantic if you mistime the final traverse. The zawn lies between a soaring north cliff and a shorter overhanging south cliff. Polished boulders, as big as barrels, rumble between these black walls during storms. At the base of the north face, there are scooped-out basins in the rock floor. These have been formed by the sea spinning the boulders like quern stones before tossing them higher into the zawn from where they tumble back in the biggest pinball game in Cornwall.

On a fine evening last week, the sun was clear in the western sky, yet its light fell only on the seaward end of the north face. The great boulders and the main cliff never catch the sun. At the back of Botallack Zawn, where the walls are a bare ten feet apart, there is an undercut cave scooped out by boulders as big as garden sheds. Coarse sand fills the bed of the cave. No ferns or lichens grow on the walls and a constant stream of fresh water cascades on to the black rocks down a jagged crack known as The Dungeon. A huge boulder is jammed halfway up the neck of the zawn and from its base a line of quartz stitches its way down the rock like trapped lightning. This is a hard place, hooded and crowded by its dark walls. Yet, on this summer's evening the green slopes above the zawn glowed in the light from a setting sun. Ruby-red stonecrop draped the ledges and outcrops of rock and the air was full of the scent of wild carrot. Two hundred feet below, in the heart of the zawn, it was already midnight.

The Cornishman 1986

Botallack hooked me into Cornwall in the summer of 1965 when I first walked down a dusty road to the famous Count House Folk Music Club. The club was just getting on its feet.

The 'resident' singers were John the Fish and Tel Mann. The club was owned and managed by Ian Todd and John Wood who lived with their families in the adjoining mine captain's house of the old Crowns Mine. I walked through the door of the Count House one fine summer's evening and walked into several years of fun as a resident folk-singer. I had barely a dram of talent but Irish blarney and Scots brass saw me through. I could manage three shaky guitar chords on a good night. I recycled constantly about a dozen songs, told stories and smiled a lot.

During those early years of the original Count House, a stream of leading folk performers showed up often out of nowhere. They included Ralph McTell, Bert Jansch, Jacqui McShee, Gerry Lockran, Noel Murphy, Jasper Carrott and Donovan. Local talent emerged, not least in the form of Brenda Wootton who in time became an international star and great Cornish ambassador. Regular local guests were Iris Gittins and Pete Chatterton from St Ives, and John Sleep and John Hayday (later of Folk Cottage fame) from the Newquay area.

Of those talented performers who came through the doors, Mike Chapman was a main man. Mike materialised from the dark mist of a Botallack evening dressed like a cross between Dylan and Donovan. Ian Todd and I groaned – lookalikes were commonplace in those days.

We asked Mike to do one number. This was our insurance against untested 'itinerant' performers. He blasted the roof off, of course, with the powerful driving guitar style that he had made his own. Self-effacing as always, Mike started to leave the stage after that one number. The packed Count House went wild. I had to crowd-surf to the front to tell Mike to keep going. He did and the rest was Count House and Cornish folk music history.

Mike Chapman went on to become an international performer though he remained always his cool unassuming

Yorkshire self. Ralph McTell went worldwide and far beyond *The Streets of London* while staying close to his much-loved Cornwall. The Todd and Wood families sold the Count House after a year or two. Brenda Wootton and John the Fish picked up the baton in a big way and shaped the booming Cornish folk scene. I knew that my lack of talent and growing disinterest would take me nowhere and, besides, I was tired of singing sea shanties and songs full of shoals of herring about which I knew nothing. I took off to the real thing. No one sang at sea.

North Coast Zawns

There are deep dark zawns on the Tinners' coast of Penwith
between Levant Mine and Cape Cornwall. Two of these have
a particularly strong appeal for me. One is called Freedom
Zawn, the other, Echo. These are not traditional given names.

They were conjured up through rock climbing. Both of
these zawns have opposing walls of dark slaty rock shot
through with quartz and other intrusions. These walls are
nearly fifty metres in height. Freedom Zawn's walls stand at
right angles to each other and form a huge corner. The walls
of Echo Zawn face each other across a ten-metre gap and
form the gorge-like elements of a true zawn.

I stumbled across both of these splendid hellholes by
happenstance during random wanderings about the cliffs.
Freedom Zawn I first spotted from the deck of a crabber some
miles offshore although it took further onshore exploring to
locate it. No one had ever climbed on the gloomy walls of
these zawns. At Freedom Zawn in 1994, during a dry May,
my old Yorkshire mate Mike Raine and I climbed nine new
routes, all of them hard and technical. It was the era of a lib-
erated Nelson Mandela. Hence, the 'Freedom' tag. We even
called one of the routes 'Nelson'. As always, Mike did the
real work of leading each route. I belayed him and followed,
secure in the presence of the rope snug to my harness and the
fact that if I fell, I would be held from above. I knew my
place.

At Echo Zawn several years before, I had climbed across
the east-facing wall followed by my friend, Graham Hobbs.
The traverse into the zawn gave fine well-protected climbing
on solid rock but the exit up the back wall was via a wet and
loose groove of flaky rock, mud and grass that gave me some
pause. We never went back to sample the huge west-facing
wall. Other things intruded; for me, it was work abroad, and
in Graham's case, a fatal illness.

During the next twenty-five years, no other climber exploited the zawn's climbing potential. I kept Echo Zawn in mind until a chance mention while climbing on the distant Rame Head tempted the great climber and mountaineer Pat Littlejohn, ever-hungry for pioneering, to Echo Zawn. I followed Pat up a brace of exhilarating routes on the west-facing wall. Soon after, other new routes fell to local climbers Andy March, Sara Scaife and Nigel Coe, good people to be with in a place like Echo Zawn.

Echo Zawn is particularly appealing to aficionados. The zawn is not easily located, until you are at its very edge, where thrift and grass abruptly give way to thin air; the tipping point. The westering sun lights up the upper section of the wall. An enormous freestanding monolith partly blocks the mouth of the zawn. It looks as if it has been lifted carefully into place. I dubbed it 'The Cenotaph'. Rounded boulders swathed in multi-coloured algae stud the bed of the zawn.

Such places are nobody's idea of Heaven, but climbers sometimes get a touch of Zawnitis; it is incurable. Symptoms include a willingness to abseil down fierce walls of rock into low tide sumps (a close knowledge of tidal movements is essential) and then to climb back out, only to do the same again. This may seem certifiable to most, but a Cornish zawn is a minuscule inversion of high and wild places, fairly exclusive, certainly uncrowded, a strange half-sea world at the cusp of onshore and offshore, a fabulous place of perverse beauty and – though you may not believe it – of delight.

CAPE CORNWALL

It was a breezy summer this year, but it takes a real winter's storm to remind us that Cornwall is first in line for the big Atlantic depressions that track across millions of square miles of ocean. Cape Cornwall takes the weather on the nose and in the early hours of last Saturday morning, you could tell there was a real storm in progress despite it being calm at sea level.

There is often a night-time lull during big storms; but you can still hear the deep and persistent roaring of the wind high overhead and the matching roar of water breaking on the shoreline.

At dawn, the wind came back to earth. Low water coincided with first light. The rocky outliers of the Brisons were ringed with boiling surf. There was a rout of broken water all the way down The Ridge, the mile-long reef that runs southeast to the rocks of the inner Greeb. Off Land's End, a matching line of white water laced the shoal ground from the Longships to the Kettle's Bottom reef. Storm waves are extraordinary in the true sense of the word. Each one is a potential killer pushed on by the one behind until Cornwall stops it in its tracks.

A few miles to the north, a squall ghosted in towards Pendeen Watch. The wind pressing ahead of it shaved the crests from the biggest waves without diminishing their mass. Long ribbons of foam streaked the surface of the sea and a lone seal surfaced for an instant amid the white water. Farther out, a brace of gannets cruised steadily upwind towards the Brisons, where great wings of spray flared to either side. The sea surged halfway up the cliff at Kenidjack Castle's headland and then drained back like quicksilver. Great slabs of storm cloud filled the sky, the air was fresh and sharp, and for a thousand miles out there was more energy on the loose than it takes to light up London.

The Cornishman 1985

Thirty years ago, Cape Cornwall was my responsibility; my downright duty – especially when there was a gale of wind. This was in the days when all coastal lookouts were still under the control of the Coastguard Service. I was a paid 'Auxiliary' coastguard at the time. In November 1985, on the day of the big wind described above, I was on early morning watch at Cape, an eight-hour stint perched on the seaward slopes of the hill, head to wind in what felt like a garden shed.

The main equipment was a chart and a hand held two-way radio. I think there may have been a kettle. At times, it felt like being at sea.

Watches on the Cape were always 'interesting' because they were staged during big storms. Main watches for auxiliaries were at Porthgwarra's Gwennap Head on the south coast of Penwith where the 24-hour lookout was a luxury pad compared with Cape's little Tardis.

Cape watches were straightforward all the same. The job was simply to keep watch and to alert Falmouth Coastguard Ops centre of any untoward events out there in the baleful ocean. I remember fighting my way along the approach track to the Cape in the early hours, feeling totally exhilarated even when I had to haul myself up the steps half on my knees to the lookout in the full force of that raging storm. I was thinking, 'This'll make a nice piece for next week's *Cornishman*'.

SENNEN:
PEDN-MEN-DU AND THE LONGSHIPS

During the past few weeks throughout Penwith the fog has
come and gone like Banquo's Ghost. From Godrevy to
Pendeen to the Longships and Tater-du, the lighthouses have
been sending out their lament. On land, fog is a minor prob-
lem of navigation for motorists; a test of good sense and
patience conducted along white lines and between high stone
hedges.

At sea, fog is a very different matter and most seagoers
would sooner face a near gale with maximum visibility than
dense fog. In busy shipping lanes, even the most sophisticated
radar may not always identify an approaching super tanker
over the final five hundred yards of a collision course. At sea,
a fog signal has a crudely practical intent. It is the last resort
of close-quarters navigation; the loudest warning shout you
will ever here.

In autumn, the Cornish sea is at its warmest and the
humidity of the air is so high it can result in several thousand
tons of redundant moisture seeking an identity.

Fog is one certain way of being noticed. It is also an
essential ingredient of Celtic romanticism, although the word
'mist' is more often used as an inaccurate but more lyrical
substitute for 'fog'. You can waste your life waiting for fog to
clear. Yet, between shoreline and cliff top, the changing pat-
terns of fog can be fascinating. Last week on Sennen's Pedn-
mên-du headland, the sun pierced the fog at times and illumi-
nated the cliff. For a few hundred yards to either side of these
sudden bursts of light visibility was minimal. The Longships'
foghorn was moaning like a steamboat's and the fog shifted
constantly between Mayon Cliff and Syntax Head. As if to
compensate for such muffled colours, a pair of Red Admiral
butterflies settled for a moment on the bare cliff face, bright
as jewels against the sea-stained granite.

The Cornishman 1985

At Pedn-mên-du, a sequence of clean-cut walls and corners starts from sea level at the northern end of the cliff. It extends above a wide and gently rising platform to a final landward gully at the southern end. The central section of the platform is a safe fifteen metres or so above sea level, although it is not the place to be in big storms. A blowhole which sent a random geyser of water high into the air, once pierced the platform. You trod warily past, when even a short sea was running below. Some years ago, a huge storm collapsed the outer section of the blowhole, leaving yet another sliced-off corner in the lower cliff.

Rock climbing at Ped-mên-du started in the 1940s when the Cliff Assault Wing of the Royal Marines took over cliff training from the Commandos' Mountain Warfare Training cadre. The Marines climbed a number of impressive lines and post 1940s several Marines, now civilians, continued to climb alongside leading civilian climbers. They turned cliffs such as Pedn-mên-du into some of Britain's most popular climbing venues.

There has been excitement other than rock climbing at Pedn-mên-du. One searingly hot summer's day I was at Sennen with a group of climbers including my old friend Toni Carver of St Ives. We noticed two anglers on a ledge below the level of the lower cliff. The sea was fairly lively but unthreatening. Toni was tackling a hard face climb while I belayed him. At one point, I called up to Toni that the anglers would have to be careful. The tide had changed and, as is often the case, the sea state had changed with it. A sizeable swell had picked up out of nowhere.

We were safely above the sea, beyond a series of rising ledges. We heard the boom of a big wave striking followed by a sudden muffled shout. The two anglers were a hundred yards offshore, their arms flailing in the tearing water of the back wave that had swept them from their ledge.

I lowered Toni down through the safety clips he had placed on the route and, as other climbers gathered, we went as far as caution allowed down the sloping ledges towards the sea. Someone made a fruitless attempt at throwing a climbing rope to where the men were being swept in and out, but the onshore wind simply blew the rope back.

This was a desperate situation. We could see that one of the men was going under. His companion was trying desperately to keep him afloat. We learned later that they were a father and his fifteen-year old son and that the father was the weaker of the two.

I had noticed a small Sennen boat passing by only minutes before the pair had been swept from the ledge. The boat was still in sight but moving steadily away. Now, we mustered a united shout, a dozen climbers bellowing as one and waving their arms in the air. It seemed unbelievable at the time, but the boat turned suddenly and headed back. The boat was the nineteen-foot *Gloreen*. It was owned and skippered by local man Nicky Hards whose fourteen-year-old grandson was with him that day.

Nicky Hards later described how they had no idea what the climbers were shouting about but had headed back to the scene anyway and had quickly spotted the men in the water. Nicky said: 'It was lucky they were outside the breaking water. There was a big swell close in. When we reached the older man, he was going under. We had to pump a lot of water out of him on the way in.'

Both of the casualties survived. Later, the father described in graphic detail what happened: 'We were a good twenty feet above the sea, laughing and joking one minute and the next thing, it hit us. We seemed to be under the water for ages and when we came up, we were right out in the sea. It was terrifying.'

As a journalist, I had found myself in the middle of an event that combined near catastrophe, luck, quick thinking, commitment, fear, generosity and gratitude, a potent mix out of which I filed a strong news report. Nicky Hards was a quiet self-effacing man who had turned back out of human regard, even though he did not know why at first. Sometimes, good things happen at sea when good people are about.

Pedn an Wlas
Belerion and The Land's End

Beyond Sennen Cove and those bare-knuckled cliffs at Pedn-
mên-du, the coast runs on to Land's End, the symbolic focus
of Cornwall's dwindling peninsula. The name 'Land's End' is
commonplace. The name in Kernewek, the Cornish language,
is Pedn an Wlas. The Romans called the headland Belerion.
To sailors of old it would have hardly mattered which of the
beetling headlands of this 'Seat of Storms' was the symbolic
Land's End. Each headland was a potential hazard to sailing
ships caught against a lee shore. Even today, a close view of
Land's End from the sea adds a sharper edge to the headland's
mystique.

For the land-based visitor that mystique is irresistible.
Land's End has attracted pilgrims for centuries. The great
Elizabethan traveller, Celia Fiennes, visited in 1698. Fiennes
established a public access precedent when, after going as far
as she could to the edge, she wrote, 'I clambr'd over them as
farre as safety permitted me.' In modern times, the same com-
pulsion has drawn great numbers of people to the Land's End
complex where tourism has distilled the history, the romantic
traditions, myths and legends of centuries into a potent brew.
As always, however, Cornwall hides many of its secrets
below our feet, unseen and unreachable by most. Beneath the
northern promontory of Dr Syntax's Head, within a narrow
cavern that slices through the headland, sea-polished boulders
like dinosaur's eggs nestle eerily in the raised galleries of
ancient seabeds.

Atlantic Edge 1995

Southeasterly Force 9

There is a long way round Land's End
When beating from the north.
Do not wear too briskly past the Light,
Let her roll and rascal west by south
A good sea mile or two to get it right,
To hold the sea at arms' length, and then,
Wear her, point by point, hard through the rout.
Hold to the turns that wrench her keel,
That bury her in flame and foam.
Let her roll and let her rise and heel,
She'll turn at last and find a straight road home.

OFFSHORE

Beyond

It makes me sick to think of it,
The stink of it, the thick of it,
The wretched retching sink of it,
The sea.

People are sentimental about fishing and its iconography.
Boats turn in harbour bristling with the emblems of their
trade. They are like war machines. Their gear is always sub-
stantial, their engines growl like bears. They edge slowly
down harbour and through the harbour gaps and into the open
sea, picking up speed until they fade into the distance and
leave the shore watcher wondering.

We lean against the quay the long day done.
The sea that cracked our bones, its fury spent,
Whimpers at our bows. The people stare.
They wonder at what goes on out there.
They wonder at the life played out and whether
Beyond the quay in the timeless other,
The place of tide and weather, we are truly gone,
Beyond the stone's throw of their vision.

There is only one way to cope with this wrenching from the
land. The mind adjusts to immediacy; the imagination shapes
miraculous catches; resignation is shrugged on as boots and
oilskins are shrugged on. You get on with it. There is no way
back until the days are done. You embrace the peculiar but
often exhilarating exclusion from everyday life and count
down the hours, without longing.

Bound Away

We ran north, our hearts undone
By a longing that robbed us of love, of peace,
Each gaze, now distant, fixed as one
On weather that we could not seize.
The wind may rein its squadrons in,
Yet, the sea is fit to bring us to our knees
With one rough blow. A backhanded blow;
The sea is not faint-hearted and is never slow.
There is no peace to spare.
No sweet reflective recompense,
For the wrack and ruin of the night,
The hard howl of wind, the blackened air.
No clear view to ease the mind,
No hark of comfort in the half-held light
Of squint-eyed ocean bearing down.
Yet, on we trudge into the heaving north,
Our hearts grown cold with distance, lost desire
As the dark hull of the night drives in.
The sea begins to bite;
A brute wind rises; a hard rain begins.

ISLES OF SCILLY

The Isles of Scilly belong to the Atlantic rather than to mainland Cornwall. They lie anchored within their sandy lagoons, each island seeming to draw its distinctive character from the cardinal points of the compass. St Agnes is bright and southerly, St Martin's sharp-edged in the clear northern light. Bryher is fresh westerly; St Mary's open-faced to the east. Tresco rests calmly at the still heart.

Impressions of a Landscape 1987

In 1969, I worked a winter season on the Newlyn crabber, *William Harvey*. I was fairly green in those days; winter fishing in Scilly straightened me out. We were based at Hugh Town harbour on St Mary's from where we worked the islands over a neap tide for anything up to seven or eight days. We arrived in Hugh Town from the mainland in the dark, left the harbour each morning in the dark, and returned in the dark. For some time I was completely in the dark about St Mary's and the other islands. The island boatmen, at their winter ease, showed little fondness for us; the islanders in general had a low opinion of visiting fishermen. We were there to plunder their fish; we were rough as rags; low case.

We worked French pots for winter crawfish on Biddy's Ground, the area of rough that lies immediately east of St Agnes. The pots were barrel-shaped and made from slats of wood with netting on the ends and a trap mouth on top. The skipper of the *William Harvey* was Mike Rouse, a good man to work with, a big man for a fisherman but a man with great experience and competence. I learned a lot that winter, often painfully.

Occasionally, strong gales rolled over Scilly and we would have several days of enforced leisure. Then, I saw the islands in all their stormy light and colour. Sometimes unworkable gales lost us half the trip. On days ashore, I strolled round The Garrison, the western headland of St Mary's that is joined like a hammer head to the main island by Hugh Town's sandy isthmus. A longer hike round the island was a pleasure even in the tearing wind. On days when the wind veered to the north-west, the sky was always blue and flecked with racing clouds. From Penninis Head among Hepworthian pinnacles, you could just see Land's End through the clear accurate light. These were the only times in my life that I felt something akin to homesickness, an unfair reflection on those beautiful islands.

Very occasionally, Breton vessels tied up at St Mary's Quay. The Bretons were true hard men. They rode out ferocious storms in the Western Approaches; but even the Bretons had their limits. The ports of Concarneau, Douarnenez and Audierne have lost many boats over the years. One of the worst incidents, in 1954, saw the loss of fifty-six men from Concarneau when five boats went down on Jones' Bank, sixty miles west of Scilly. The vessels were riding out a ferocious November gale. The depth of water over the bank ranges from thirty to fifty fathoms but deeper water around the edges can be a maelstrom of overfalls and cross-seas. In March 1976, fifteen Bretons were lost on Jones' Bank in similar conditions.

In Scilly when a gale was forecast and Breton boats started coming in, we knew a major storm was brewing. The French maritime forecasts were significantly better than the UK's. We used to say: 'The Bretons are in! Quick, put out more lines! Big gale coming!'

Some Scillonians, and even Cornish fishermen, were wary of the Bretons, but I liked the cheerful little men in their blue work jackets and pants, wooden clogs and *de rigeur* Breton caps. If you smiled, shared food and drink and were friendly, any language barrier was easily overcome.

The roughest wine in the world comes from the cabin of a French fishing boat. You could scrub a deck down to the bare wood with *Le Gut Rot*. For Breton fishermen, however, *Le Gut Rot* is the Breton equivalent of tea. Given the circumstances, it all tastes like home. The wine aboard the Breton boats was vile, but those men could cook.

'You come with us, Scottie!' they would shout to me and off we'd ramble at low tide to the more sheltered beaches of St Mary's where the world lay flat all the way to the horizon.

The drained foreshore seemed to lie beneath a distant sea and its crests. The Bretons quartered the rock pools and the weed-swathed reefs, buckets in hand, pick-pecking away, lifting stones, foraging in the limpid pools like a little flock of wading birds, like turnstones, oystercatchers, until they had filled the buckets with every kind of seafood you could hope to find. The air fizzed with the harsh smell of the sea and seaweed and damp salt-crunching sand. Then it was back to the boats, where soon a different smell, the aroma of rough-cut *bouillabaisse*, came drifting from the galleys. You could happily drink *Le Gut Rot*, known more elegantly as *intestinale pourriture*, along with that kind of fabulous food. You can never have too many Breton cooks oiling the broth.

In late October 1980, I shot eight tiers of nets on Biddy's Ground. Leaving nets out so late in the year was a gamble, but catches of crawfish could be very good in late autumn. I took the risk. We ran home to Newlyn to wait until the tide eased. Two days later, a friend phoned from Scilly to warn me that a 150-foot Hull stern-dragger was inside the legal limit for her size and was towing mid-water for mackerel across Biddy's Ground. This could prove disastrous to fixed gear if the trawler dragged the lines and dhans that were attached to the anchored nets. We took off west immediately. Poor weather was forecast. When we reached Scilly, the trawler was gone. We searched fruitlessly for gear. Most of the dhan lines were cut or tangled below surface. I had to tow a heavy 'creeper', a metal shaft with rows of 'teeth', across the estimated location of a net end in the hope of hooking into the net. Miraculously, we recovered all the gear without too much net damage and with a decent haul of crawfish. That was it. I brought the nets home for the winter.

WORSE THINGS HAPPEN AT SEA

Worse things happen anywhere; but the sea can be particularly 'worse'; unforgiving, random, overwhelming. The unexpected is always at hand.

On September 10, 1987, in fair weather deep off the French coast, the Newlyn fishing vessel *Sharon Corrina* had just shot one of her nets that now lay anchored to the seabed, its lines to the surface marked by red buoys. The 65 foot wreck-netter was owned and skippered by Dave Hibbert and had a crew of five. Hibbert was an innovative fisherman, a stocky likeable Yorkshireman, unassuming and sociable. He had introduced to the Newlyn fleet a way of catching dogfish that developed into a major fishery. Hibbert was known for his independence and for being one of the port's top catchers.

The *Sharon Corrina* was working many miles from Newlyn and was closer to France than to Cornwall. The vessel had been at sea for a number of days. As they headed away from their gear, the crew heard a loud bang, startling in its suddenness. They had noticed earlier what they assumed were two military planes manoeuvring above them. Now, when they looked astern they saw a spreading circle of oil and debris on the sea's surface. One of the planes had nose-dived into the sea.

When the *Sharon Corinna* headed back towards the scene, the crew realised that amid the debris was the pilot, still connected to his parachute. The pilot was dead; his injuries were obvious and horrific. The aircraft were French and Hibbert was soon in contact with the French authorities who had already been alerted to the incident by the other pilot.

Soon after, a French Naval helicopter arrived and dropped a rescue diver into the water. Time passed – for too long. A second diver was sent down and was then quickly winched up carrying the limp body of the first diver who, the fishermen learned later, had died amid the oil and debris of the crash. The helicopter left rapidly. The coastguard asked Hibbert to retrieve the body of the pilot from the water and to wait for another helicopter. With some reluctance, the crew retrieved the body and wrapped it carefully in a tarpaulin. When the helicopter arrived, it approached the *Sharon Corrina* from astern in the accepted fashion, trailing a hook and line, with which the fishermen would secure the pilot's body.

There was a very big swell running by this time and as the helicopter made its approach, the hook-line snagged on the *Sharon Corrina's* mizzen mast. The vessel was now fast to a helicopter in the rise and fall of the sea. Dave Hibbert described the scene: 'It was unbelievable. We were pitching heavily and here was this helicopter caught fast to our mast with static electricity burning down the wire as well.'

Rob Page, one of the *Sharon Corrina* crew, shinned up the mast and freed the tangled wire; a remarkable effort. Even now, the incident was not over. The helicopter made a second run but the heavy hook at the end of the dangling wire smashed through one of the *Sharon Corrina's* wheelhouse windows. A third effort went smoothly and the body of the pilot was finally lifted into the helicopter.

Later that evening, a French Navy minesweeper arrived on the scene. An officer crossed to the *Sharon Corrina* in an inflatable, thanked the crew for their help, and presented them with a small silver dish by way of appreciation.

The crew of the Sharon Corrina were skipper Dave Hibbert and crewmen Steve Crossley, Craig Rogers, Rob Page, Ian Campbell and Terry Freeman.

In response to my Press inquiries, the French authorities refused to confirm that the incident had taken place.

THE SEVEN STONES

The notorious reef that lies a few miles north east of St
Martin's Head on the Isles of Scilly is a country in its own
right. No one can raise the flag on the Seven Stones, but you
cannot ignore them and during big tides the Stones will show
their heads at low water in one way or another. Pollard, South
Stone, Flat Ledge, North East and Flemish Ledges with their
minor reefs make up the Seven Stones, great fists and slabs of
sea-polished rock, black, striated, and marbled-white like
sharks' teeth.

In 1967, the Pollard rock had its ears clipped by the
super-tanker *Torrey Canyon*. The Pollard struck back with
dire results to the shores of Cornwall and Brittany. Now, in
the dim, seething undertow of the reef, the great ship lies in
pieces and skin-divers say that no weed grows on her.

The main tops of the Seven Stones stand out for several
feet at low water springs, the Pollard Rock most of all. You
rarely see it from a vessel close-to although in ground seas the
swell can break suddenly across the Pollard and always much
nearer than you think. It's like being snapped at.

The tides round the Seven Stones are hard and sudden in
their streams and even in flat calm the ebb takes off like a
river through the sea. It can turn a boat three times about. Yet
there is good lobster fishing here, especially within the central
area of the Stones themselves, a tight, working quarter known
as *The Village*, best suited to small easily handled vessels.
Larger fishing boats have been known to work here but not
without paying a high price. The Seven Stones do not move
aside for anyone.

Impressions of a Landscape 1987

ONCE BITTEN: SEVEN STONES REEF

On a windless day of ground swell,
When the sea was smooth as pearl,
We drifted east on an ebbing tide
To where Pollard Rock broke sudden
A berth away.
Its monster back rose with great snappings.
The swell flamed into foam and maelstromed
And the boat, like a stung horse, leapt.
She rolled along the roof ridge
Of the Pollard's burst sea house
And sluiced to the glide of safe water,
Over west.
Our hearts hammered.

We remembered the day; Tuesday March 28, 1967, ten days
after the grounding of the supertanker *Torrey Canyon*. In a
broad stony field at Trewellard, on the north coast of the
Land's End Peninsula, Mrs Betty Sykes, her young son and I
were scattering nitrate pellets, preparing the cleared and raked
ground for planting potatoes. It was like some biblical parody;
scattering nitrate 'seed' instead of seed corn.

I worked for a time for Betty and her husband Donald,
who farmed a difficult handful of acres across that hard country. We knew all about the grounding of the *Torrey Canyon*. It
was the talk of the western land.

The tanker was nearly a thousand feet long and had a
draft of nearly seventy feet; it had been lengthened, 'jum-
boized', during the oil boom years of the 1960s, thus doubling
its capacity. It was carrying 100,000 tons of oil and was a
lumbering catastrophe waiting to happen. It was American-
owned, sailed under a Liberian flag of convenience and was
charted by British Petroleum; the usual suspects. As much as
thirty-one million gallons of oil leaked from the ship and

spread across the sea and on to the English and French coasts. Tens of thousands of seabirds were killed and foreshore life was destroyed. It took years for a recovery that may still have left certain marine life depleted irreparably.

The tanker had struck on March 18 and a scramble to contain its haemorrhaging oil was well under way. Containment was disorganised and misdirected. The immediate tactic was to dump 10,000 gallons of 'detergent' that was sprayed, poured and simply jettisoned willy-nilly across the sea and beaches. Detergent was a cosier name for what was in truth highly toxic 'solvent emulsifier' that did more damage to marine life than the crude oil might have done.

After ten anxious days, the Prime Minister of the day, Harold Wilson, his intent even more focused perhaps because of his close connections with the Isles of Scilly, ordered bombing of the still visible wreck in a bid to ignite the oil. The Royal Air Force and Royal Navy dropped over 160 bombs and over 5,000 gallons of kerosene on the *Torrey Canyon*. All of this had little effect. Rockets were even fired at the wreck in the wake of an embarrassing 'miss' rate of a quarter of the bombs dropped. Finally, the planes dumped 1,500 tons of napalm, the notorious and vicious 'anti-personnel' mix of gelling agent and petroleum that until then Britain had denied stockpiling. All of this firepower had little effect and the wreck finally broke up and sank among the towers of 'Lethowsow', allegedly part of the mythical Land of Lyonesse, while its oil bled away in a long and deadly slick across the sea.

On that March day in 1967, it was the first successful strikes by the warplanes that made our field day memorable at Trewellard. It was a grey day, but the sky and sea were a vast canvas, the visibility crystal clear. Betty Sykes called out suddenly and there, far out across the sea, a great plume of black smoke mounted rapidly into the sky. There were flashes of orange flame within the surface smoke. It was an unforgettable image of the sea on fire although not for long.

BETTER A GALE OF WIND...

There are things worth seeing at sea... none better than in clear air beneath blue skies although this is not the way of the Atlantic in its restlessness. The sea stirs things up. Storms apart, the sea is at its worst in fog. Fishermen say they would rather have a gale of wind than fog, especially in the 'steamship' track, the common highway for cargo carriers, for reefers, for oil tankers, as they plough past Land's End and The Lizard, or up Channel. Oil tankers are great blind beasts in fog, hampered within their lumbering momentum, not keen to turn away for anyone within the time-honoured code of port side to port side when approaching bow to bow. Even with radar, fog is an uneasy hazard. Radar may register blind spots at times. You can be tracking the hefty blip of a super-tanker ahead of you only to have the blip disappear, or merge with the central screen 'clutter' the closer you get.

We were hauling nets one day in a flat calm, a few miles east of Scilly. There was blue sky above, but a band of very low fog, thick as the proverbial bag, engulfed us. Visibility was barely a boat's length ahead. When a fishing vessel hauls gear, that vessel is effectively anchored to the seabed. It is a 'hampered' vessel. Other vessels should steer clear. However, there is no certainty that this rule will be followed.

Trawler skippers tie the onboard ends of trawl warps, the cables that are attached to the net on the sea bed, to the winch drums with light twine. There is always unused warp on the drums but the ends are made fast lightly so that, in extremis, if the skipper feels that he may be at imminent risk of being run down, he can unbrake the winch and give the vessel full ahead in a bid to escape collision. Then, the warps run out freely, the fixed twine at their limit breaks and the warps dis-appear over the side letting the vessel speed clear, hopefully out of harm's way. A lost trawl can be recovered. Collision with thousands of tonnes of supertanker may not be recoverable from. On line-hauling boats, a sharp knife is always at hand, in case the nets or lines need to be cut quickly.

On that eerie fog-laden morning, I was checking the radar closely and could see the blip of a vessel approaching from the direction of Land's End. It was on a direct line to our position. It was several miles away but when I checked again soon after, it proved to be travelling at a remarkable speed. I kept my knife very close and warned the crew that we might have to cut the nets outboard of the winch. The approaching vessel might have been a speedboat of some kind, a Gin Palace taking advantage of the flattened sea with heedlessness as to the poor visibility.

I stayed close to the radar with some anxiety. The approaching blip seemed to accelerate towards us. The fog was in our faces yet the bank of fog was so shallow you could look up and see blue sky. The approaching vessel was now a mere half mile away, still at speed and heading straight for us. I was on the point of cutting the net and gunning the boat away when the Isles of Scilly helicopter roared by overhead, and over our thudding hearts.

I knew the pilot and bumped into him a week or so later. He had seen the tip of our mast protruding from the low fog and could not resist a visit.

'The passengers thought it was great.'

'Oh, yes...'

The best thing to see at sea is a 'fog eater', a rare phenomenon that occurs as a white arch in dense fog. It has a faint rainbow aura at times and it is caused by sunlight burning through. The arch steadily expands and, within it, the fog clears like a tunnel of light until all the surrounding fog melts away on a freshening breeze. Worth seeing at sea for sure...

FOG EATER

Grant us a gale of wind, instead
Of this blind bearing down
Of fog upon our anxious tread.
It clouds the mind, obscures entirely
Steel-clad monsters mustering ahead.
We edge across the sea, peer through the murk
Of midday's sodden gloom, the half-dark.
Until: a spark of light and the fog eater gapes.
It props its pearly arch and grows,
A gateway glow of sunlight shining through.
The wind rises too. The sea begins to break,
Blends green with silver as the light streams in.
The fog eats out. The blue begins.

BISHOP ROCK

The roughest ground in Scilly lies around Bishop Rock to the south west of St Agnes. Here the islands give way grudgingly through a string of iron-hard reefs and shoals to an ocean that is frantic with tide and ground swell. For most of the year, these Western Rocks are in the grip of wind and tide.

In Broad Sound, where the ground rises abruptly at Jeffrey Rock and the Gunners, the swell increases and then eases for a time until the tight channel between the Bishop Lighthouse and Flemmings Ledge is reached. Here, fierce tidal currents and Atlantic swells tear each other apart in a rout of tumbling sea.

Hauling gear can be harder than usual for several miles beyond the rout when spring tides are grudging on the slack and dhan buoys are dragged under for most of the tidal cycle. The buoys surface for only a short time at slack water and sometimes not at all.

Making passage into Broad Sound from the west on a big following sea can be heart stopping, even in a sizeable vessel. This is the Atlantic's Gate where the depth of water would barely cover a house and where wrecking reefs with names to match their menace lie to either side – Hellweather, Gilstone, Tearing Ledge, Retarrier, Crim and Zantman; names to savour while they set your teeth on edge.

The sea is so fast here that a vessel may lose way as the stern lifts on a following wave and the prop spins uselessly in thin water, only to bite again as the great sweep of the wave surges on and the next one builds astern. At such times, the Western Rocks hardly bear looking at where they run off to starboard beyond the streaming stem of the Bishop to Gorregan, their black teeth in a fury of white water and seething tide.

Ahead lie Annet and St Agnes, dark smears of land beneath a frantic sky. The air is harsh with the smell of the

sea while the roar of the wind and the hiss of each racing
wave seem to stifle the heartbeat of the boat's engine as it
counts the nerve-wracking minutes towards safe water.

Impressions of a Landscape 1987

STANDING TO GEAR

Stepped in dark waters west of Zantman's
On a high heave of ocean without storminess;
The sea was menacing, amassed,
As if the wind might burst suddenly
Through its tensed surface, shattering glass.
It was nightfall. The Atlantic was above.
Below, to all quarters. The sunken buoy was slow
To rise from a hard tide of seething water.
We were unblinking; but nothing showed
As darkness closed and the vast ocean shuddered.
A hard-helmed circle I made then let the chains slide
As she wore towards the islands
Through the sea's grey light and glide.
The swell was like a helping hand astern
Where the buoy welled up on the slack,
Then slid back, overwhelmed.

I worked tangle nets to the south west of Bishop in the 1979
and 1980 summer seasons. No one had shot for crawfish in
those deep quarters at the time. Decca Navigator was our only
positioning aid. It used a system of electronic signals, classi-
fied as red, green and purple 'lanes'. The intersecting points
of the 'lanes' indicated the position of fishing gear. Decca was
not very accurate south west of the islands because of the
extremely wide band of the green lane. The system could be
inaccurate up to a mile, which made locating dhan buoys very
difficult, especially in wild weather.

The Atlantic weather was uncertain during those late
years of the 1970s. West of Scilly, the swell remained high

and constant, workable enough in quiet weather but as soon as a front approached, the sea became frantic. Hauling nets from fifty fathoms with the kind of primitive winches we had in those days was not easy. I lost a number of nets and found few fish in spite of widespread searches using an old Breton chart that showed a few areas of rough ground.

The dreamt-of Eldorado materialised only once; a cluster of high pinnacles as far west as I dared go. I marked the ground as 'America' in my catch log. During a rare quiet spell, we hauled a decent catch of crawfish and even lobster, not often seen in tangle nets. The fish were small and a touch spent but this was the only worthwhile haul in several frustrating weeks. The persistent fronts toppled in once more and I took what was left of my wrecked gear and my sanity out of there. It was a desolate quarter in every way.

HAULING AMERICA

This seemed such hopeful ground to raise;
To mark one final track out west.
I sought no promises, no praise,
No farther, brothers, than this, I said.
We've wasted time enough and sweat
With these hard-heaved nets, these tatters.
When wind and tide prove fair
We'll haul the world's edge; unstitch
Each grudging kindness from this grim place
Of stones and fetters, bones and rusting hulks,
Then turn our faces east from such ill luck.

There was an intriguing footnote to those stormy summers. Several years later, I was working as a reporter for *The Cornishman* newspaper in Penzance. One day, in the office, a call came through to me from a staff member on the front desk.

'I've got the *New York Times* on the phone,' she said.

'They're doing some report or other about scientists investigating an increase in the height of waves in the Atlantic during the late 1970s. They wanted to know if anyone could talk to them about it. I told them I knew a man who could...'

It was a fascinating moment. The reporter from the *NY Times* was delighted to find someone who had been out in the Western Approaches during the period of the scientific survey. I was more than able to confirm that there had indeed been particularly heavy weather during the summers of 1979/80 and that big swells were relentless.

The Last Roundup

During the 1970s, a major fishery developed in Mount's Bay. The target was mackerel, a fish that had served local fishermen in a sustainable way for generations.

Traditionally, mackerel had something of a bad press compared to other pelagic favourites such as herring and pilchard. In Scotland, it was considered a poor fish whose feeding grounds included the end of sewage outfalls. As a child in Scotland, I remember fishing off St Andrews in a small row boat and catching anything up to thirty or so individual mackerel using a line with a single hook. When I took the fish home, my mother would scold and then my father would dig them into the garden as raw fertiliser.

Things changed for the Scots when their herring industry took a dive in the 1970s. The Scots had already influenced Cornish fishing. The traditional method of catching mackerel in Cornwall was to trail a single 'spoon' hook behind the boat. A catch was counted in single fish. The story is that several Scottish Marines training with the Cliff Assault Wing in the 1940s came from North East fishing ports. They brought back from leave, fishing lines with several feathered hooks on each one, the 'Scotch Feathers' that produced lines full of fish during good feeding conditions. When I first came to Newlyn in the 1960s, the Cosalt chandlery on the Strand still sold 'Scotch Feathers'.

The Cornish soon improved on the Scotch Feathers method and by the winter fishery of the 1970s, local boats were using anything up to thirty or forty hooks per line. The feathers were gone. Small sleeves of coloured plastic replaced them. This was a perfectly sustainable fishery. A top Newlyn boat with four skilled crewmen could catch anything up to a thousand stone of mackerel in a day's fishing, the fish being in prime condition.

The winter fishery flourished for several years with

dozens of Cornish boats, from twenty-foot 'toshers' to fifty-foot summer netting boats making a fair living. When the huge extent of the mackerel shoals became known, coincident with the banning of herring fishing in the north, the Scots came calling.

Three Scots herring boats, a pair trawling team and a purse seiner turned up unannounced in Newlyn Harbour in the mid-1970s to a cold welcome from locals. No Newlyn fishermen would speak to the Scots at first and they soon moved across the bay to Penzance's inner harbour. I never doubted that the skippers of those vessels had been carefully recruited. They were canny, personable men of great experience and I am sure that their fellow Scots had tasked them to assess the potential for industrial fishing of the South West mackerel. They had already checked out the huge shoals that were flooding across Mount's Bay. The Cornish skipper for whom I worked at the time was forward thinking and thoughtful. He and I broke the embargo and called in on the Scots' boats, with a judicious bottle of good whisky. I was there to 'translate'. We soon saw what was about to come.

The dire warning locally was that these Scots raiders would soon be followed by half a dozen more, but for anyone who knew the Scottish industry or had seen a hundred-strong Scots' fleet moored off Ullapool for the weekend, the gates were already open. In no time, dozens of vessels, including pair trawlers, massive stern draggers from Hull, lately driven out of Icelandic waters during the 'Cod Wars', and, the most ruthlessly efficient catchers of all, Scottish purse seiners, were hammering the mackerel in Cornish waters.

The boats came from Shetland, Peterhead, Buckie, Hull and Grimsby and they did not let up until they had fished the mackerel shoals to pieces. The only foreign vessels in evidence during that 1970s bonanza were Russian, Ukrainian, Polish, Romanian, Bulgarian and Dutch freezer factory ships moored off Falmouth. They were not fishing, but buying and processing the fish that British vessels caught. They were essential to the fishery, yet there was still paranoia among the non-fishing public that these were foreign vessels 'robbing'

UK fishing grounds. The foreign crews of the factory ships were also spending tens of thousands of pounds in the shops and pubs of Falmouth. The fishing carried out solely by British boats was ruthless, relentless and often against the rules. The Scots and Ukrainians ran much of the marketing through offices ashore. They were not over generous.

I worked occasionally on a pair trawling team in the early 1980s. I remember a quiet winter's night, deep to the south east of St Agnes Island, when what was probably the swan song of the big mackerel fishery took place. About thirty boats had been hunting for twenty-four hours without luck when a seiner hit a shoal of small mackerel. The rest of the boats, pair teams, sterners, and pursers all closed in on the seiner.

This was in the dark of the night; thirty vessels, each ninety-foot upwards in length, the pair teams and mid-water trawlers with their gear out, quartering the narrow bounds as close to the seiner's huge spread of net as they could go. It was like a seaborne dance but without any contact whatsoever; a remarkable exhibition of close quarters boat-handling. I remember leaning out of the galley window and watching the floats of the purser's seine net as we skimmed by, only metres away, while a stern dragger cut across our bows. It was all to no avail. The seiner hauled thirty tons of small fish. The rest of us had none and the fleet dispersed. The Shetlanders, the Scots and the east coast boats headed off on their long trips north. The great Mackerel Klondike of the 1970s was effectively over.

This is how fishing works. But fish have tails and no one 'owns' them. These days we should be careful of what we wish for, especially when the Scots are on the case. I can say this without fear of being accused of prejudice...

Once, they ran like rivers through the sea, those fish
And our one thought was on their hunting;
We took the lot...

ONSHORE:
SOUTH FACING

NANJIZEL, CARN BOEL, ZAWN REETH

The great headland of Carn Boel lies to the south east of Land's End. Two massive granite blocks split by a steep gully of broken scree crown the headland. This pattern of hardness and decay is repeated between Land's End and Gwennap Head where wind and sea have worn the coast down to the bone. Headlands and bays alternate in a sequence that has produced some of the finest cliff scenery in Britain.

Carn Boel is an airy enough place most of the time; but in the hard westerly winds that followed this Easter's rain, the caves and fluted chimneys that split the granite blocks were sounding like pitch pipes. At the base of the cliffs, huge seas wrecked themselves on the hardest rocks of all. Between Carn Boel and Zawn Reeth, at the western end of Nanjizel Bay, the low shoreline is broken and decaying. Banks of soft and mossy earth rise above the shoreline and are held together by wild flowers during spring and summer. Sea campion and stonecrop are already well established this year.

Across Nanjizel Bay, great swells, each one measuring a thousand yards from headland to headland, raced into the shore. Where they broke at the western end of Zawn Reeth, the sheltered pool that lies inside the reef had its usual group of seals. Today there were six of them. They drifted nonchalantly in and out of thick clumps of seaweed and across the sandy floor of the channel. They watched us watching them – and with as much curiosity. In the tearing water beyond the reef, where ebb tide and wind-driven waves clashed, two young bull seals rode the tumbling seas effortlessly.

Human intrusion has driven seals from many beaches and sandy coves where their young were once born with some chance against stormy seas. What this has cost in a possible reduction of the number of seal pups surviving to adulthood is hard to judge although on this stretch of coast, in the sea caves of Bosistow beyond Carn les Boel, seal pups are still born on the silver sand. From low on the cliff face, you see them drift lazily through the sheltered channel between the mainland and the huge rock pinnacle of Bosistow Island and you hear the haunting echo of their song.

The Cornishman 1985

Porthgwarra: Gwennap Head

Gwennap Head outclasses Land's End in many ways, not least by its lack of gratuitous entertainment and by a sometime sense of isolation. It is known also as the Fishermen's Land's End because it is the most southerly limit of the peninsula and is the point where the tidal stream divides, one arm flowing east through the English Channel, the other flowing north into the Celtic and Irish seas.

The headland's traditional name is Tol-pedn-Penwith, the 'holed headland', the Tol being the huge funnel-shaped blowhole or 'sink' that lies at the eastern end of Chair Ladder cliff. This blowhole is a classic coastal feature that is more common on limestone coasts, although there is a similar sink called the Devil's Frying Pan near Cadgwith on The Lizard and another known as the Round Hole at Trevone near Padstow. Such features are caused by waves slowly eroding a cavern at the base of a cliff where the rock is weak and friable. Eventually the cumulative effect of storm waves results in a collapse of the upper plug of earth and loose rock, thus forming a blowhole. The sequence has been repeated at many points on the coast of the Land's End Peninsula, but many of these features eventually collapse and form the open clefts known as zawns. Tol-pedn is a genuine blowhole however and has a land bridge between the cliff edge and the gaping hole in the ground.

Chair Ladder cliff is over two hundred feet high and extends for a thousand yards to the northwest of the blowhole through a sequence of walls, buttresses and pinnacles that sea and wind have honed and polished into fantastic shapes. A mile offshore, the Runnel Stone Buoy warns of a string of dangerous rocks and ledges that lie due south of the cliff. These are the two outermost Runnel Stones themselves and the rocks that lie between them and the shore – Poldew, Carn Stone, Lee Mean and Lee Ore.

During big tides and strong westerlies this is one of the most impressive seascapes on any stretch of coast in Britain. There is a channel, navigable by small vessels, that leads along the base of Chair Ladder. It is best avoided in heavy weather, although running through here in a well-found boat with a big westerly swell astern gives a very different view of Cornwall than you get from the back of the Land's End bus.

The Cornishman 1985

The Gwennap Head coastguard lookout stands on the summit of Chair Ladder. The lookout is now in the hands of the National Coastwatch Institution. The name Gwennap is thought to relate to a local family who may have had rights on the headland. There are suggestions that Tol-pedn was a lookout position for centuries. A signal station was located there prior to 1800 and the facility probably remained active until the ground floor building of the present lookout was opened in 1910. The upper storey was added in 1956 to increase the range of view. The lookout operated full time until 1994 when twenty-four hour watch keeping by paid auxiliary coastguards ceased. The NCI took over watch keeping in 1996.

I worked at Gwennap as an auxiliary coastguard in the early 1980s. Watches were mainly at Gwennap although I covered the Cape Cornwall Lookout during extreme storms. There was an almost seagoing sense about night watches except that the deck of the ops room at Gwennap did not move underfoot. In a strong onshore gale, the big reinforced Perspex window that looked out to sea directly in front of our chart table used to bow in and out like a wobble board. When the wind reached Force 9 or above, we were allowed to evacuate temporarily to below decks in case the window blew in. It never did; but the thought of this actually happening still amuses and horrifies me.

Our duties at Gwennap extended beyond watch keeping. We reported weather statistics to the Met Office base in Plymouth by recording a series of quite complex readings that we took every three hours. These included wind strength, rainfall, and visibility. Gauging visibility in the dark of night was often problematic, especially on moonless nights or in fog.

When required to, we activated the fog signal at the unmanned Tater-du lighthouse, which was over four miles away to the east. The lead lighthouse for the western land was Lizard. If fog came in at Lizard the coastguard there would instruct Gwennap to activate Tater-du. This had to be done even if there was clear visibility at our end of Mount's Bay.

To start the Tater-du fog signal we used an odd contraption that resembled something out of Doctor Who's back catalogue merged with a fruit machine – all buttons and coloured lights. There was a phone connection from Gwennap to the inside of the lighthouse at Tater-du. Having activated the signal you lifted the handset and listened until you could hear the moan of the seventy-two speakers at the lighthouse. I wondered sometimes, especially in the early hours, what my reaction might be if a disembodied voice answered.

I was familiar with Chair Ladder cliff as a climbing venue. There is no other cliff quite like it in Cornwall. It confronts the ocean like the facade of a grand cathedral. Towers and pinnacles, fluted columns, gargoyles, finials, mouldings, tracery – all of these features are embodied in Chair Ladder's Gothic facade, often in surreal yet familiar forms.

The 'Funnel' blowhole that gives the headland its traditional name excited the interest of Victorian botanists and topographers. There are stories of Victorian 'adventurers' entering the cavern. Some became trapped by the incoming tide. The great 19th century naturalist and devoted explorer of Penwith, John Thomas Blight, described how two over-eager plant gatherers were trapped by the tide at the base of The Funnel. One of the pair could swim and managed to fetch several fishermen who hauled the trapped man up with ropes. An even more determined botanist once clambered down to the base of the cliff while the tide was in and tried to swim into the cave, but the sea dragged him back. He tried again, successfully this time, and later wrote, with some insouciance, *...I gathered a fern, Asplenium marinum, held it in my mouth and swam back...*

St Levan:

Black Carn Zawn

Black Carn Zawn is a rocky inlet that lies just under a mile to the north west of Porthgwarra. Its walls rise in broad shelves of granite like the tiers of a coliseum.

At its seaward edge, a huge perched boulder watches over the zawn. Viewed from the lower cliff, the boulder resembles the head of an old woman complete with mobcap, ferociously hooked nose and jutting chin. Her profile is like an illustration from Mervyn Peake's *Gormenghast*.

The wind and rain of centuries have wrung the old witch's neck to a thread and she may nose-dive into the sea one of these days.

Last Sunday, in the burning light of June, the heat was at full blast along this coast. The sun was near its highest point of the year. On the upper cliff, wild flowers tumbled over themselves with excitement.

Great sprays of yellow kidney-vetch spilled down the rocks and crowded round the sea campion, thrift and pink stonecrop. On one narrow shelf, the shallow soil was bone dry; a near drought already in spite of weeks of rain. Here, the flower heads were already dying back in the heat; yet, in cool shadowy clefts amid the surrounding boulders, fresh blooms still glowed with colour, their roots sunk deep into water-bearing moss.

At the base of the cliffs, there was no swell although a rush of white water pumped in and out of the narrow channel as the tide fought against the outfall. Offshore, the sea glittered like ground glass. Fifty feet above the tide line amidst a wilderness of bare rock the remains of a herring gull lay jammed in a crevice; bones and pure white feathers only, the whole displayed in a strange dynamic form as if the bird had flown into the rock at full speed and been trapped there, its wings outflung.

The Cornishman 1986

MINACK AND PORTH CHAPEL
IN WINTER

On Christmas Day over half an inch of rain was recorded at
Gwennap Head on Penwith's south coast. A few degrees less
and we might well have had a seasonal white Christmas. As it
was, between Christmas and New Year, at least one day of
glorious sunshine revealed a pale dusting of white on the
inland hills of the peninsula.

Last Friday, the night skies cleared to reveal a pale moon
while an easing of the raw north winds produced what meteo-
rologists call 'nocturnal radiation' leading to 'sublimation of
the water vapour' – hoar frost by any other name. Such frost
cuts like a knife, breaks ground, and may even split granite.
For a time, early in the day, it makes sodden ground fit to
walk upon. Around Porthcurno and the Minack, there was
thick ice on the sunless tracks, yet, on the beaches at Porth
Chapel and Porthcurno, sheltered as they were from the wind,
it was as warm as a spring day in the bright sun.

Frost and Fire; the sun's heat eased the iron-hard ground.
Between the Minack Theatre and Porth Chapel Beach,
bunched heather and gorse overhung the seaward edge of the
track that runs across the headland of Pedn-mên-an-mere.
Frosted trails of dead grass glittered like bridal veils. Here
and there, the sun's warmth had loosened the ice cover where
thin trickles of water flickered beneath.

Fangs of ice hung from the dripping cliff and below the
headland the granite walls shone like gold in the afternoon
sun. Visibility was sharp and clear to the horizon. Off Lizard
Point, the cluster of rocks known as The Stags seemed to float
above the sea's surface. Looking to the south everything was
bright. Yet, on north-facing slopes inland, where the sun's
rays could not reach, cold shadows bred freezing air. The
grass and bracken were stiff and brittle and a few campions
hung their limp heads as if the frost had wrung their necks.
The Cornishman 1986

Today, in 2017, the beaches at Porthcurno and Porth Chapel are much as they looked all those years ago. Little seems to have changed at Pedn-mên-an-mere and Porth Chapel, although, directly below the headland, a massive rock fall of several years ago has reshaped a sizeable section of cliff that was unstable anyway. Unseen changes are often at sea level.

On the summit of Pedn-mên-an-mere you will still find the iron base of a radio mast that dates from 1902. This is all that remains of what was known as the Marconi Mast. For years, even locals thought that the mast was a legitimate piece of telegraphy equipment installed by the Marconi Company. In truth, the mast was an early exercise in industrial espionage by the Porthcurno-based cable communications group, the Eastern Telegraph Company. The ETC, a commercial rival of Marconi, felt threatened by Marconi's new 'wireless' technology that they feared would supplant undersea cables. The Pedn-mên-an-mere mast was fitted with radio aerials that were used to eavesdrop on radio traffic from Marconi's experimental transmitting station on The Lizard. It was dismantled on the outbreak of the First World War on the orders of the War Office because of its potential for 'misuse' and potential 'espionage' – by whom was not specified; an exquisite irony all round.

Porth Chapel has its own undersea memories for me. One summer's day, in the distant 1980s, I jollied out of Penberth in an eighteen-foot punt with two young local rascals, Billy Chapple and John Clemens.

We had borrowed a 'mini' trawl from those estimable cove men, Bobby and Teddy George. Complete with neat little wooden otter boards, it was a perfect miniature of the traditional Granton gear used by Newlyn sidewinder trawlers of the day. My companions were enthusiastic and intent; I was a touch sceptical. I worked on big boats; they were determined to impress.

It was a beautiful June day; the sea was calm and clear as gin beneath a cloudless sky. We shot the tiny trawl in the middle of Porthcurno Bay. I remember lounging in the bows as the sturdy outboard roared under the heft of the trawl that we could see through clear water laid out perfectly on the sandy seabed astern. I kept one lazy eye on random landmarks and soon realised that we were not making an inch of progress and were firmly anchored to all that golden sand by the weight of the trawl.

Dismay and disgruntlement all round; but, hope sprang eternal and we tootled off round Ped-mên-an-mere and The Carracks to try our luck off Porth Chapel; in shallower water and close to an undersea reef known as School, or Shoal, Kelynack. The reef is thought to have been named after a local man who, many years before, had been a pilchard huer on the cliff and had mistaken the purplish colour of the reef for a shoal of pilchards. Derision and immortality of a kind followed. Our luck was no better.

This time the mini trawl did move across the ground and we did haul a bulging bagful – of assorted seaweed, two dabs and a mini crab. But, on such a day… in such great company… in Paradise.

St Loy:

Porthguarnon Cove

St Loy's Cove, two miles west of Lamorna, is where the
Cornish spring begins. Last week, on a still and misty day, the
wood that runs inland from St Loy's beach was like a stage
set arranged carefully as if for a spring rite. Daffodil buds
unfurled their golden-crowns and covered the floor of the
wood. Within a few yards of the roadside, snowdrops, prim-
roses and a solitary crocus, out on parole, had found a place
among the green and golden ranks. The trees were still leaf-
less and winter-worn, however, and on the western slopes
above St Loy's Cove there was a rout of smashed timber from
recent southeasterly gales.

West of the cove, the coastal path climbs steeply above
the cliffland, while a lower track leads towards Merthen
Point. Beyond St Loy's wood is an open landscape of granite
cliffs and huge boulders through which the surefooted can
find a way. It leads to the shoreline from where smooth boil-
erplate slabs lead back at a gentle upward angle to the base of
St Loy cliff below Trevedran.

At its eastern end, St Loy cliff falls back into smaller
tiers where isolated blocks of granite rise from the green
slopes like rough Cornish equivalents of the sculpted heads of
Easter Island. The main cliff is non-tidal and is set back from
the sea. Its central feature is a smooth, domed buttress of perfect grey granite. It is over one hundred feet high; there is a
diamond-shaped slab at its heart. Today, the cliff was running
with water. Its grey face matched in colour the low banks of
fog that lay offshore. In a few weeks from now, this entire
area will be a wild garden of vivid colour. Already the honey-
suckle is in leaf and further inland, amid the fields and paths
above Porthguarnon Cove, there were occasional violets and
periwinkles while the ever-present daffodil buds waited in the
misty air ready to get their act in first.

The Cornishman 1985

Tater-Du and Boscawen

This is a wrecker's yard of rock and iron,
Where wind and sea went mad together;
Now is the ease of the commonplace,
Calm upon the dead forever.

To the west of Lamorna, below the quiet fields of Tregiffian and Boscawen Rose, lies a wrecking coast of rock and iron. At its heart is the black cliff of Tater-du, a greenstone outcrop, a cool apéritif before all those miles of sun-baked granite that run west to Land's End.

Rock walls and terraces descend to the sea from the eastern edge of the cliff. Offshore, lie The Bucks, twin tidal rocks that are set far enough into the seaway to pose a hazard even for local vessels. A lighthouse was built on the rocky foreshore here in 1965, two years after the wreck of the Spanish coaster, the 640 tonne *Juan Ferrer* with the loss of eleven of its fifteen crew.

The coaster ran aground in a southwesterly gale off Boscawen Point just west of Tater-du. Dense fog hampered the searchers, ashore and afloat. The main search was concentrated to the west of the actual wreck due mainly to a fragmented Mayday call from the stricken *Juan Ferrer* stating that the vessel had run aground near Land's End. A wide-ranging search of the western coast proved fruitless and was called off. The wind decreased and the sea eased to a near calm; a dense fog persisted.

Only the instincts and local knowledge of Penberth men, Bobby and Teddy George, brought resolution. After the official search was suspended, the pair drove to Tregiffian Farm on a hunch. As they walked down the lane towards Tater-du they could smell the fumes of diesel fuel leaking from the stricken vessel. When they reached the coast, they met three bedraggled Spanish sailors struggling along the top of the cliff. The captain of the vessel was later rescued from where he clung to floating wreckage.

During the 1960s, I worked a small mackerel tosher called the *Fairlight*. It was owned by John Nicholls of Newlyn. John worked for Trinity House and maintained as part of his duties the unmanned Tater-du lighthouse. The *Fairlight* had been one of the wooden lifeboats on the *Juan Ferrer*. It had somehow drifted away from the wreck in one piece. The little boat was salvaged by a St Ives fisherman who renovated it and equipped it with a bow dodger and cuddy and a trim little engine. It was christened the *Fairlight* and eventually came into John Nicholls' ownership.

There always seemed to be a short run of fish under the cliff just west of Tater-du, in the area where the *Juan Ferrer* had been lost. It was uneasy there all the same, even in quiet weather, as if taking the *Fairlight* back to its mother ship was a step too far.

A touching sequel to the wreck of the *Juan Ferrer* came in 2016 when a headstone was placed in a Penzance cemetery above the unmarked grave of four of the lost crewmen from the vessel. The headstone was funded from donations from members of the public through the inspiration and good work of the Heritage Team at the Penlee Lifeboat Station.

Eighteen years after the wreck of the *Juan Ferrer*, just before Christmas 1981, sixteen other souls were lost in the wrecking of the Penlee lifeboat *Solomon Browne* and the coaster *Union Star*. The wrecking occurred near Boscawen Point in the steep-sided cove that lies between Zawn Gamper and Chough Zawn just to the west of Tater-du.

On that dreadful night with a southwesterly gale gusting to hurricane Force 12 raging across Mount's Bay, the great rounded boulders in the bed of the cove could be heard grinding together under the onslaught of the massive sixty-foot waves that roared into the coast.

Today, metal shards of the coaster are still jammed between boulders. The forrard part of the vessel lies amid the rocks and, far back in the dripping throat of the cove, a twenty-foot section of hatch coaming lies twisted like screwed-up cardboard. The cove is like a bombsite with the broken hull of the *Union Star* at its centre. The tidal granite is stained with rust. Seaweed that dries black in the sun covers the boulders in the bed of the cove. Green algae covers the remnants of the *Union Star's* hull. Only round the edges of the zawn do the warm colours of granite re-emerge and, on the cliffs above, multicoloured mosses and sedge merge with the passive greens and yellows of the upper cliff. In quiet summer weather, this seems a scene awaiting an artist's palette.

The eight crewmen of the *Solomon Browne* were lost after making epic rescue attempts that stand beyond the judgement of ordinary mortals. The eight people aboard the *Union Star*, including two children, were lost also. The story of the lifeboatmen's heroic work in first rescuing four of the people aboard the *Union Star* and then making a final bid to evacuate the remaining four crewmen has been told often enough. A powerful account of the tragic events is recorded in the book *Penlee: The Loss of a Lifeboat* by Michael Sagar-Fenton.

I knew all of the crew of the *Solomon Browne*, especially the fishermen among them. For a short time in the summer of 1969, I was a shipmate of the coxswain, Trevelyan Richards. Charlie, as we knew him, was relief skipper for a six-week spell aboard the Newlyn-based longliner, the *MFV Kilravock*, which was owned and skippered by Michael Hosking of Porthleven. Charlie took over when Michael had to stay ashore for a time.

The *Kilravock* was a sixty-five foot wooden vessel, Buckie-built, a splendid Scottish sea boat. I swear that you could stand in the waist of that vessel head to wind in a half gale and you would hardly feel her move.

We worked ground sixty or so miles west-nor-west of the Isles of Scilly where a small fleet of Newlyn longliners, including the *Rose of Sharon*, *Spaven Mor* and *Girl Pat*, made week-long trips throughout the late spring and summer. We were looking for such fish as cod, haddock and ray with lucrative skate being our main target. Ling were always seen as a useless by-catch that went for fish paste in those days.

Sometimes we went up channel, deep off St Ives, fishing for turbot by day on gravel banks. They were all great trips that were mainly successful but occasionally frustrating. We left harbour already in debt through payments for fuel, ice and food and had to make decent catches to pay for it all and still pay the seven-man crew. It was all part of the 'glorious uncertainty' of the fisherman's trade.

Longlining involved shooting thirty baskets of line, each one carrying over two hundred hooks that were hand-baited with slices of fresh mackerel. It took nearly four hours to shoot the ten miles of joined lines and then anything up to fourteen or fifteen hours to haul them. You do not need a calculator to work out how much sleep we had when you add in the gutting and icing down of the fish, clearing decks and dealing with unexpected delays. Add to this the shared night watches during which the vessel was kept close to the big wooden dhan and its blinking 'winkie light' that marked the end of the lines. All of this on decks that often rocked and rolled in tumbling seas and howling winds. Three shots in a week's trip; by the second shot, sleep became a distant promise. We broke through a barrier of endurance somehow.

Trevelyan Richards was a tall man, remarkably so for a fishermen. Most fishermen are fairly short. A low centre of gravity is an advantage on the heaving deck of a fishing boat. Charlie moved about the deck like a cat, his long legs bent at the knee. He had command; he held a crew together well and was liked greatly. He was not a man to back off in the face of monstrous fate and risk.

This is a graveyard of the good,
Whose deaths all weaknesses dismiss,
Where brave and bold are words defined
by chaos, monstrous fate, and risk.

KEMYEL CREASE
AND LAMORNA

The five-acre wood known as Kemyel Crease is a distinctive feature on the coast path between Mousehole and Lamorna. Last week, in strong southeasterly winds and with a hint of snow in the air, the trees at Kemyel gave welcome shelter. The wood is said to have been first planted with conifers in the early 20th century. Later, in 1940, local farmer Hartley Giles added deciduous species. The trees acted as windbreaks for small meadows, or 'quillets' that for many years yielded violets and early potatoes. Now, only the walled outlines of the quillets survive among the crazed tangle of trees.

Among the salt-resistant Monterey Pines and cypresses that lend Kemyel Crease its 'forested' look, Mr Giles planted ash, sycamore, horse chestnut, poplar, privet and a few mimosas. A fine stand of flowering cherry trees survives at the western end of the wood.

At present, in cold February, the wood is bleak and dark though even a near gale seems to make little impact here. Only the cypresses sway uneasily where they stand tall and mast-like among the heavier conifers.

Leaving the shelter of Kemyel Crease for the open coast to the west was like leaving harbour. The air was full of wheeling gulls while, in line with the low cliff top, stiff-winged fulmars dipped in and out of the chanks and small bays. These tough little northern petrels moved south from Scottish waters between the wars, feeding on fish offal dumped from southbound fishing boats. They were first known as St Kilda Hawks after the remote islands west of the Hebrides where they nested. Lowestoft fishermen heading home from the herring grounds first reported fulmars off North Cornwall in the 1930s. Nowadays they are common-place around Southwest Britain. Their defences include the swift ejection of foul-smelling stomach oil to deter predators and any humans who get too close.

On shore, there were no signs of land birds until inland from the headland of Carn-du, a green woodpecker rose like a game bird from the dead bracken. Its bright colours stood out against the pale wintery landscape like a harbinger of spring.

The Cornishman 1985

In 1985, I wrote of Kemyel Crease woods, 'Even a near gale seems to make little impact here', a comment that deserved to be blown away. Written in 1985 it was nothing if not naive. In January 1990, a ferocious gale ripped the wood of Kemyel Crease apart, felling mature conifers and choking the under-growth with debris. Even today the wood seems crippled, though it is not forlorn. There is still a dramatic contrast between the shadowy cloisters of the wood and the exhilarating openness of the coast path to either side.

Cornwall Wildlife Trust has owned Kemyel Crease since 1974 and much work was done after the 1990 storm in managing the routed timber and in replanting. The ill wind also blew in some good. The fallen trees left skylights in the tree canopy through which the sun penetrated and enlivened the once sterile ground beneath. Flowering plants and shrubs flourished among the wrecked timber and broken walls.

Beyond Kemyel is Mousehole where the coast is a turning point into the inner confines of Mount's Bay and where the village seems to absorb the coast into its amphitheatre of granite houses that rises like a terraced cliff from the cove-like harbour. Offshore lies Mousehole Island, St Clement's Isle, a marker for outgoing and incoming Newlyn boats. The seaway changes here as you turn into a freshening sea when you're bound away or ease out of the open mouth of the bay towards home when bound in across the reach of water known for centuries as Gwavas Lake, past Low Lee Buoy, past Penlee Point and all its noble ghosts.

BOUND IN

Sometimes, night air in autumn falls
Bone-chill on Gwavas Lake,
Where only the rumble of our wake
Disturbs the silent sea's content,
As Newlyn shines its eerie light
On Gwavas Lake at the black midnight;
While, at our backs, gargantuan,
A harsh and overarching sky relents
From threatening us with harm.